Advance praise for Backyard BBQ Financial Planning!

"Owen tackles a critical subject for entrepreneurs—what to do with the wealth you create. All too often for most Canadians it's an afterthought. An easy read with important content for those who recognize that a goal without a plan is just a wish!"

—Peter Kinkaide

"Whether you're starting your career or right in the middle of it, this light read will provide valuable financial insights, as well as prompt thoughtful discussion about how to manage personal wealth. Owen strips out the complexity, focusing on the fundamentals you can use today. Great read!"

—Cory M. Sutton,
B.Mgt, CPA, CA, CFE

"A comprehensive introduction to the basics of financial success for ordinary Canadians in a conversational format. A very valuable addition to everyone's financial planning arsenal."

—G. Thomas Carter,
BA, MA, JD

"An interesting and informative book that will help anyone along the road to financial literacy—a wealth of information covering all the basics you need to know from starting in the workforce, starting a family, buying a business, financial planning, and estate planning. A must read for any budding entrepreneur who is interested in starting their own business."

—Rob Quilley
FCPA, FCA

Backyard BBQ Financial Planning!

Backyard BBQ Financial Planning!

Owen Jackson   CPA, CA

Jackson Financial Media

Copyright © 2015 Owen Jackson
Backyard BBQ Financial Planning
First Edition, Paperback, 2016

All rights reserved. You may not use or reproduce by any means including graphic, electronic, or mechanical, photocopying, recording, taping, or by any information storage retrieval system without the written permission of the publisher. The only exception is using brief quotations embodied in critical articles or reviews.

ISBN: 978-1535252034

ISBN: 1535252030

Printed in the United States of America

DEDICATION

For my family

Chapter One

Making Plans

Paul decided somewhere between high school and college he really didn't want to pursue a career within the corporate culture. "That's for stiffs in suits," he said. "I'm not interested in being one of those guys who never gets out of a cubicle—not happenin'!" He was serious, too—and, no matter what his mom said, she knew he would never face a judge in a courtroom as an attorney, or sit behind a desk all day pushing a pencil. Nope—according to Paul, he had bigger and better plans for his life.

Plumbing.

Plumbing? What kind of kid out of high school decides to be a plumber? Unless, of course, he's carrying on a family tradition—or, he has the good luck to work his way to the top by being an apprentice on the bottom. According to Paul, it's a kid who knows how to turn a dime into more jingle in his pocket. A kid who knows he wants to make money.

It's an understatement to say his mom and dad weren't thrilled with the idea—they had big dreams of their only son attending college—a 'good school' his mother called it—which could provide the opportunity for a good life. But Paul was having none of it.

Plumbing it was.

****

Fast forward. Paul did exactly what he said he would, and he trained as an apprentice plumber, climbed the ladder, and married the love of his life by the time he was twenty-five. Much to his parents' surprise, he was making a darned fine living, and Paul and his wife were in a good financial position. At least for the time being—Paul had ideas for starting his own company, but he knew doing so would take planning. Unfortunately, he had no idea of how to go about taking on such a project for his future—he was always an 'in the moment' kind of guy, and he didn't have the chops to create a plan to get him where he wanted to be in five years. Ten years. Thirty years.

When you think about it, you have to give Paul credit for knowing he needed a plan at the tender age of twenty-five—that's an understanding many people twice his age don't have, and will never figure out. But, as with anything new, there were upfront costs involved when hiring a professional to help him. Three-hundred bucks an hour was average, and he anticipated many hours of work for the right CPA or financial planner. Besides, trying to get on a reputable CPA's docket was next to impossible.

Enter Dan. The guy who lived next door.

Chapter Two

Movin' on Up . . .

Sometime during the summer, Paul and Mandy decided it was time to move. They tossed around the idea of starting a family, but put it on hold until they had their own home. So, the search began, and they wound up purchasing a great little starter home on the west side. Nothing fabulous—a three bedroom ranch, two baths, and a good sized kitchen. As soon as they walked in the door, both knew it was the home for them, and they made an offer that day.

Move-in was a month later.

Paul immediately wanted to improve the property in order to increase its value, and there were several things needing sprucing up. His wife, an avid fan of home improvement television shows, had the guts to take on a renovation, and they laid down a plan for incremental changes. First up was landscaping—weeding. Planting. A new fence. The only time available was the weekend, and it was on a steamy, fateful, Saturday afternoon that Paul met the man who would change his life while he was weeding the flowerbed on the southeast side of the house.

"Hey, Neighbor!"

Paul straightened, not sure if the voice were speaking to him. He listened for a moment, then returned to weeding, deciding the greeting was for someone else.

Again, a bit louder. "Hey, Neighbor—you there?"

Paul stuck the trowel in the ground, brushing his hands on his pants. "I'm here!" The voice came from across the high board fence—too high for him to see the man with the deep voice. "What can I do for you?"

"Just want to introduce myself—we wanted to give you a couple of weeks to get settled before officially welcoming you to the neighborhood."

"Thanks—we appreciate it! My name is Paul . . ."

"Dan. Dan Carpenter. My wife's name is Linda . . ."

"Well, Dan Carpenter, it's nice to meet you . . . Mandy is my wife, and I know she'll be thrilled to meet someone. After we get settled, maybe we can barbecue—what do you think?"

"Sounds like a plan—but, you better get back to it before it starts to rain!"

The men left it at that and, within ten minutes, Paul was in the house, watching torrents slash against the window.

"Do you want some cookies? Just out of the oven . . ." Mandy slipped her arm around her husband's waist, joining him watching the rain.

"Have you ever known me to pass up cookies?" He grinned at his wife, and leaned down to give her a gentle kiss. "Do you like living here?"

"Of course, I like living here! What's that supposed to mean?"

"Just that owning a house is a lot more responsibility—I know we're up for it, but, I have to confess, it's a little scary."

Mandy laughed, giving him a squeeze. "True, but once we get everything the way we want it, I think you'll be sure we made the right decision."

"Hey—I forgot to tell you I met our neighbor!"

"Which one?"

"Right next door—the grey house."

"Cool—I didn't see anyone here . . ."

"He wasn't—we talked over the fence. Not for very long, though—so, I invited his wife and him over for a barbecue once we're settled. Okay with you?"

"Yep—fine with me." Mandy slipped out of the comfort of her husband's arm. "Do you want milk?"

****

By the end of August, Paul and Mandy felt as if they lived in the neighborhood all of their lives. The front yard was done, but there was still work to do in the back. Mandy managed to reno the kitchen almost by herself, and they thanked their lucky stars Paul was a plumber. His skills alone saved them a chunk of money—and, with the kitchen completed, they were ready to host their first get-together.

Dan and Linda accepted their invitation the week before and, as Paul slapped chicken and steaks on the grill, his guests appeared at the backyard gate. Mandy only spoke to Linda over the fence one or twice—same with Paul and Dan—and it was nice to put a face to the voice.

"Smells good already!" Dan headed toward the grill as Mandy and Linda headed for the kitchen.

"Nothin' better than grillin' on a hot summer day!" Paul checked the grill temp, then opened a well-stocked cooler. "Beer? Soda?"

"A beer is fine, thanks!"

"Light or Guinness?"

"Guinness..."

"Same here..."

****

Chapter Two—Movin' on Up

Twilight suited Paul and Mandy—it was the time of day when they could relax, enjoying each other's company. Evenings were cool as summer waned, and the two freshman homeowners were still getting used to the idea of having a place of their own. The whole responsibility thing continued to be a stickler for Paul, although Mandy didn't give it much thought. She was more of a 'free spirit' as her mom used to say—she'd rather think about such things later, knowing somehow everything would work out.

"You cold?" Paul thought he detected Mandy shivering, but he wasn't sure. "I'll grab your sweatshirt . . ."

"No, thanks—I'm fine. Besides, I have you if I get too chilly!"

Paul grinned, realizing for the millionth time how lucky he was to be married to her. "Well, okay—but if you get cold, let me know." Mandy flashed a smile, leaned back in the wicker chaise chair, and closed her eyes.

Paul, too, loved the filtered light of dusk—it made him feel as if he accomplished something that day, and it was his reward. He didn't have much time to relax since the barbecue with Dan and Linda, nor did he tell Mandy about his conversation with Dan after they went in the house that night.

"Babe? You awake?"

Mandy opened one eye. "Of course, I'm awake!" She shifted in her chair, wrapping her arms around her. "Why?"

"Nothing, really—it just occurred to me I never told you about my conversation with Dan the night we had them over for the barbecue . . ."

"So—what did you guys talk about?"

"Sports mostly, but he asked me a question I hadn't given much thought to . . ."

Mandy waited for her husband to continue. "And?"

"He asked me my definition of 'financial success' . . ."

"Financial success? What happened to sports?" Mandy teased. Paul shot her a look telling her he was serious. "Okay—sorry. What did you say?"

"His question took me by surprise, and I didn't really have a good answer—and, that's when he told me his definition—*financial success is when we don't have to worry about money, anymore.*"

Mandy sat up a little straighter. "Are you worried about money?"

"Not really—well, maybe. I just don't want to be in a position of when I look up some day, I realize we don't have much to show for our hard work."

"We have the house . . ."

"True, but after talking to Dan, I realize we need to do quite a bit more planning in order for us to be comfortable."

"Like what?"

Paul grabbed a beer from the cooler, lifting the bottle in a mock toast. "At first I thought I was just being a worrywort, but he made me realize we need to start now if we want to reach our goal."

"Which is . . ."

"Financial independence . . . I think. At first I thought financial planning was for people who were already at the top—not a young couple like us. But, you know, it makes sense. He told me Canadians should be much more concerned about their financial futures than they are."

"I believe that—look at my parents . . . they were always scratching for money, and it seemed as if they never had enough."

"I know—Dan said there are a whole lot of folks who are in a bit of panic when they reach their fifties, wondering how they will throw things together within a couple of years."

Mandy thought about her father who passed when he was only sixty-two. "What's sad is those people will never have the opportunity to retire . . . Daddy worked hard and, when he died, I know Mom had no idea how she was going to carry on without him. Without his income. Of course, she didn't have kids at home anymore, so I suppose it was a little easier. But, no matter how you cut it, carrying on wasn't easy for her."

"That's exactly what Dan said—many people often give up on retirement, let alone early retirement. They just hope their health holds out . . ."

Paul and Mandy sat in silence, thinking about their own situation. For the first time in her life, Mandy was beginning to realize the importance of planning for the future.

"So . . . where do we start?" Mandy looked to her husband for the answer. She was clear she had no idea, and he was the math brain, anyway.

Paul launched into a complete recounting of his conversation with his neighbor, making sure to leave nothing out. He told Mandy the questions he asked Dan, but his most important questions were how they could get started, as well as how much they would need to retire. Dan responded by telling him most Canadians with a clear title residence as well as a retirement fund of two million rarely have financial problems. Of course, there was always the possibility they would worry about money anyway, but the truth was there was no need.

"Two million? Holy cow—how on God's green earth are we going to save two million dollars?" Mandy couldn't believe what she was hearing! Two million dollars? A tiny of thread of doubt started to creep in—that amount of money seemed pretty far-fetched to her.

Paul read her feelings perfectly. "I know how you feel—I felt the same way until Dan explained how to do it. In fact, all it boils down to is simple arithmetic . . ."

"Arithmetic?"

"Yep—dig this—our after-tax income minus our living expenses produces a yearly fund. That fund, Dan said, is used to buy major purchases such as houses, cars, or cabins—whatever. What's left is our nest egg for emergencies and retirement—of course, that nest egg can grow if we invest it."

"I get it—but, we can also lose that money if the investment goes south . . ."

"Let me finish—Dan said living expenses have two key roles. One, they reduce the size of the yearly fund. Two, they also impact how big our nest egg needs to be. Big spenders have a pretty severe challenge, and frugal people have a massive advantage."

"But, what about expenses, major personal purchases, and investing? I didn't hear you mention anything about them . . ."

"Good question—it was interesting, because Dan commented few Canadians seem interested in planning for their futures—they just want the big house, jazzy car, and

Chapter Two—Movin' on Up

expensive vacations. Lot's of expensive vacations . . ."

"That's not who we are," Mandy interrupted.

"Agreed—and, I told Dan that. Here's what amazed me—there's a good chunk of Canadians who chase the dream job that requires higher education, and they wind up with a big, fat mess. No job. Massive debt."

"That's why I didn't want to attend school anymore after graduating from university . . . I didn't want to start my life having to owe a bunch of money."

"Same here—it's why I chose to be a plumber instead of being the guy in a suit."

Mandy looked at her husband fondly. "And, you look fabulous in jeans—you're not a suit kind of guy!"

Paul noticed Mandy blowing on her hands. "You're cold—let's go in."

"Okay—but, one more thing. It sounds great, but how are we going to achieve a two-million dollar dream?"

"Not sure—Dan said he has some homework for us . . ."

"Homework?"

"That's what he said . . ." Paul jumped up and crossed to his wife, pulling her up from the chaise. "I'm as new to this as you—but I think it's worth checking out, don't you?"

"Yes—and, as soon as possible!"

"Well, that's a surprise—I thought you might be a little hesitant. Talking about finances used to be off limits . . ."

"The operative phrase is 'used to be' . . ."

"Apparently—okay, give. What changed your mind?"

Mandy reached into her pocket, and held up a pregnancy test stick.

"You're pregnant? Are you kidding me? How long?" Paul couldn't keep an already huge grin from widening to ear to ear.

"I suspected last week—now we know!"

"When's the due date?"

"Late May, or early June—I have to go to the doc's in a couple of weeks..."

"Then I better talk to Dan—we need to get going now!"

"Yep!" Mandy eased into her husband's arms, feeling his warmth. She knew the timing was right...

Chapter Three

Homework

"You're kidding, right?" Mandy looked at Dan, unsure if he were pulling her leg. He wasn't. What he was asking them do to sounded nothing less than silly.

"Nope—visualization. It's easy—ready?"

Paul glanced at Mandy. "I guess . . ."

"Okay—close your eyes, and imagine the two of you sitting on one side of your kitchen table, side by side." Dan waited for several seconds before continuing. "You're looking across the table at couple who looks a lot like you—Paul and Mandy with more wrinkles, more grey hair, and probably a bit heavier." He waited for the visualization to take form. "Of course, this is the two of you about thirty years from now—financial planning is like making a fair deal with this 'couple.' It's going to be fair to you, and you need to be fair to them—the couple. If you have a good income, surely you should have a reliable car and enjoy nice holidays, but it doesn't need to be a Lamborghini and 5-star resorts."

"That's good," Mandy commented. "It's not our style, anyway."

Dan smiled. *They have what it takes*, he thought. *They'll make it* . . . "Basically," he continued, "financial planning isn't about pleasing your advisor—it's only a negotiation between you and this 'future you.'" He could see Paul and Mandy were struggling with that one. "For example—say your investment advisers performed poorly, but you don't fire them because they give you hockey tickets. Isn't that being a little unfair to the older couple sitting across from you?"

Paul spoke first. "So, our homework is to get used to the idea of reaching a fair deal with this older couple?"

"Correct—I believe you'll make 'fairer' decisions if you keep this visualization in mind while we discuss the four key components of a financial plan.

"I remember them," Mandy piped up. "Income, expense, major personal purchases, and investing . . ."

"Excellent! If you keep those things in mind, this will be a snap for you! Remember—pleasing me isn't important. Being happy with yourselves in the long run is the key."

****

Chapter Three—Homework

Remembering the couple sitting across from them turned out to be an easy exercise, one which put Paul and Mandy squarely on the road to a solid financial plan. With a baby in the mix, Paul wanted to implement a viable plan immediately, but he didn't want to impose on his neighbor, always asking his advice.

"You're not imposing, at all," Dan told him from across the fence that week. "To be honest, giving a young couple like you a little advice feels good . . . how about our place on Sunday? We can watch the game, and I'll answer any questions you have . . ."

Obviously, Paul jumped at the chance—and, Mandy could surprise Dan and Linda with news of their baby. By the time Saturday rolled around, Paul had a list of questions the length of his arm. He didn't want to overdo it, and he didn't know if each question had a simple or complex answer.

Mandy leaned over his shoulder as he sat at his desk, thinking about the following day. "Holy cow! Did you think of enough questions?"

Paul grinned. "I know—every time I think of one question, it makes me think of another. I just don't want to forget anything . . ."

"Well, if you do, he's next door—you don't have to ask all of your questions at one time, you know. Chances are pretty good you'll see Dan a lot!"

Her husband nodded, and put down his pen. "You're right—I forgot to ask you, though, what questions you have for Dan . . ."

Mandy perched on her husband's knee. "Well, I've been thinking since I want to be a stay-at-home mom, I won't be contributing to our income the same as if I had a job. Of course, I couldn't do this at first, but I could work my way into having my own business . . ."

"Seriously? Staying at home, and having a job? That's going to be a lot of work . . ."

"I know and, like I said, it won't be for a couple of years. But, that doesn't mean I can't start laying the groundwork now. What do you think?"

"If that's what you want to do, I'm all for it—what kind of business?"

"Interior Design—all I will need is space for an office."

"Makes sense to use your degree!"

"Doesn't it? Gee—all that money not going down the drain! What a concept!" Mandy hopped up, giving her husband a quick peck on the cheek. "I have things to do . . ."

"Like what?"

"Like baby shopping . . ." With that, she was out the door, grabbing her purse as she headed for the garage.

****

Dan and Linda's home reflected exactly who they were—a little dated, but as comfortable as favorite shoes. Linda had a

Chapter Three—Homework

bit of a bold streak in her when it came to decorating, but she was always careful to include Dan's tastes. He loved rustic, she loved French country—between the two, their home was inviting and cozy.

The open floor plan allowed the boys to take up residence in front of the television while the ladies prepared appetizers in the kitchen. Conversation involving the four of them quickly dwindled as they claimed their respective places.

"So . . ." Dan prompted. "We have about thirty minutes before the game starts—what do you want to know?"

Paul laughed. "If only you knew!" He told Dan of his list of questions, thinking he must sound a little bit like a nut.

"That's good! There are a bunch of questions you should ask. So, fire away!" Dan laughed, and turned the television down until the start of the game.

"Mandy and I did a lot of soul searching, and we just don't see how we can retire on my income as a plumber . . ."

"I know—and, it's good both of you are thinking about it. Unfortunately, it's a sad fact that few Canadians—other than government workers—have a decent pension. We're not saving enough—few buy significant RRSPs, and most Canadians have way too much debt. When I think of my clients who retired wealthy, most of them owned their own businesses. And, frankly, they kept their spending under control." Dan paused for a moment, grabbing a handful of chips from the bowl on the table. "The truth is many professionals have good income, but their daily spending is extreme—they also tend to spend too much on big ticket items such as houses and vehicles. It's interesting—when I think about it, I have more wealthy retired tradesmen than professionals."

"That's good—at least I'm starting out on the right foot!"

"Indeed, you are! But, look—I'm jumping all over. How about if I just give you my thoughts on income for now..."

"Sounds good to me!"

Dan swiped at his mouth, then wiped his fingers with a napkin. "I think it's a crying shame most young people's career plans focus solely on what they enjoy doing. Yes, liking your job is nice, but most jobs have disagreeable elements to them—normally, people have fun at work because they bring a positive attitude to whatever they do."

Paul nodded. "Agreed. I can't imagine going to work every day for a job I hate..."

"I personally think," Dan continued, "part of a career plan should be about what the community needs, as well as what it's willing to pay for..."

"I'm not sure I understand what you mean..."

"Just this—people obtain qualifications after years of expensive training in fields where there are no jobs." Dan chuckled at Paul's look of surprise. "Oh, yes—it usually comes as a big shock to them even though job shortages are rarely a secret."

"It's like the Madisons, Paul . . ." Mandy piped up from the kitchen. "You remember them—their son went to university for theatre, and it was a rude awakening when he figured out he couldn't make money at it!"

"Same kind of thing," Dan agreed. "And, you have to think about what you do well—my initial plan was to be a doctor. Back in the '70s, doctors seemed to have a solid income, and that attracted me. But, it turned out my talent is seeing the big picture, and I have a tough time memorizing

Chapter Three—Homework

detail."

"Really? You wanted to be a doctor?"

"I did—but, as you can imagine, learning Latin names for a bunch of body parts, as well as what to do in a wide variety of situations was impossible for me."

"I know what you mean—I couldn't do it, either!"

"My friends and family knew I had a flair for business, but I wasn't so quick on the uptake—I didn't focus on it until third-year university. When you think about it, no one wants to believe they're average—the thought being you'll be better than average at whatever you choose to do. That said, I wouldn't bet too much against the averages."

Paul looked a bit perplexed as he reached for his beer. "So, if the average owner of a used book store makes little, but the average owner of a plumbing company does well, isn't it obvious what holds more promise?"

"Exactly! Many people choose what they love, but earning a substandard income takes the shine off the apple quickly. However, you can still be a plumber, and hit used book stores on the weekend."

Paul thought back to high school, and how everyone thought he was crazy to be a plumber. "In my case, I was always building things as a kid, and I just couldn't see sitting at a desk all day. Even then, I knew obtaining a good trade was key."

"Let's take that one step further—if plumbing company owners make—on average—ten times more than their employees, you'll probably want to focus on being an owner before too long. Sure, you want to learn on someone else's dime—but ask your boss if you can help with estimating. Or, take a course in estimating."

"So," Paul asked, "how does that figure into a sound financial plan?"

"Remember I mentioned the RRSPs? Well, if you're heading toward owning your own business, I wouldn't put my savings into RRSPs—those funds can't be used as security. Instead, you may want to pay down your house mortgage because home equity is great security. Or just keep your savings outside an RRSP for now..."

Mandy and Linda joined their husbands, plates of appetizers in hand. "Then how does income fit into the big picture?"

"Good question." Dan snatched a stuffed mushroom before Linda could place the platter on the coffee table. "Overall, the engine propelling you to a great place financially is the difference between after-tax income and spending. For example, say you make $80,000 net of tax, and spend about $60,000. So multiply the $20,000 difference by forty years and that's $800,000—using that money to pay off a $400,000 home means you'll have $400,000 for retirement."

"Is that enough?" Mandy asked.

"No—I know it sounds like I forgot investment income, but, typically, it only offsets inflation. But, where things can change in a hurry is if your income were higher because you owned the company. Say you now make $180,000 net of tax—even if your spending climbs to $80,000 you will now save $100,000 a year. Forty years of that, and you're in great shape! So you'll want to get started on this path soon—the trick is to make sure you know what you're doing..."

"That's if you own your own business—I feel sorry for the guy..."

"Or, girl..." Mandy chipped in.

Chapter Three—Homework

"... or, girl who doesn't go that route..."

"It's a sad fact," Dan agreed, "lots of people aren't cut out to own their own businesses—hopefully, you are. My experience tells me most Canadians who started modestly and became wealthy, were successful business owners."

"That's where filling the community need comes in..."

"Precisely. I don't know much about plumbing, but you could look into what happens if someone has an emergency on the weekend, or in the evenings. If the plumbing companies in town are too comfortable to bother with these emergencies, you can be the emergency plumber." Dan paused to let his idea germinate in Paul's mind. "Of course," he continued, "you'll work a lot of evenings and weekends, but that kind of sacrifice can make you successful. Or, let's say people tell you although they like their plumber, they hate the mess the plumber leaves behind. You could guarantee people you will either clean up—to their satisfaction—or pay for a cleaning service to do it. By doing so, you can charge a superior rate. Even if you did pay for cleaning on occasion, you could still be miles ahead..."

Paul nodded. "It comes down to asking around, and filling a need."

"Actually," Mandy added, "Paul and I spent quite a bit of time talking about plans like this—we think it's the path we want to take."

"That's good—and, it's critically important both of you are engaged in the plan. Think about a few years from now—you have your own plumbing company and, Mandy, you're at home raising your young children. Those years are tough. Linda and I certainly went through lots of days where I was working silly hours, so her sacrifice was considerable. At times, she felt like a single mom—but, with both of you sharing the financial plan, you will know why the two of you are working so hard."

Mandy glanced at her husband, smiling. "Speaking of children..."

****

As it usually seems to happen, Paul and Dan didn't have an opportunity to get together for several weeks after the game. Mandy's pregnancy progressed nicely, but, into her second trimester, something wasn't quite right and she ended up being in the hospital for four days. By the time she got home, winter weighed in, and Mandy was relegated to bed rest until her next checkup.

"I didn't count on this..." Paul reached into their mailbox. "Nothing but bills..."

To Dan, it was clear stress was beginning to mount in his young friend. "I know it's none of my business..."

Paul attempted a smile. "Listen—right now, I can use all the help I can get!"

"Are things that serious with Mandy?"

"Serious enough—I'm just hoping we don't have anything else go wrong. But, the doc says if she takes it easy, she should be in fine shape—at least the baby is okay."

Chapter Three—Homework

Dan clapped Paul on the back. "Why don't you take a few minutes for yourself—come in for a cup of coffee!"

Paul hesitated, realizing a little relaxation time was exactly what he needed. "Deal—let me tell Mandy, and I'll be over in a few minutes . . ."

****

Mugs in hand, the two men sat at Dan's kitchen table, fresh donuts for each. Linda excused herself, leaving them to discuss the world's problems—or, at the least, Paul's problems.

"I think," Dan began, "you have a pretty good idea of how expenses can balloon out of control—and, if you're not prepared, those expenses will chew you up, and spit you out before you know it . . ."

"Man—you're not kidding. Mandy and I always try to put something away each month, but I can see if her problems were more serious, we could be out of luck . . ."

Dan placed his coffee mug on the table. "Well, based on what we talked about previously, I think we should pick up with expenses—okay with you?"

Paul grinned as he felt his body take a five-minute break. It was nice to put his problems aside for a while. "I'm all ears!" He thought for a moment. "I do think Mandy and I do well as far as expenses go—we came from humble families, and I think that helps."

Dan nodded. "I agree. But, there are some crucial things anyone starting out needs to know . . ."

"Such as?"

"Such as figure out what stuff you really need—I found out I don't really need much in my life. I don't need fancy cars, or toys that cost more than my house, and more stuff doesn't improve my life—in fact, it seems to get in the way."

"Example?"

He paused, as if trying to think of an example that may fit Paul's life. "Well, as you know, Linda and I travel with backpacks six months out of the year . . ."

"Backpacks? I'm not sure I get it . . ."

Dan grinned at the look on Paul's face. "They're small enough so we don't have to check them when we fly. We fill two backpacks with good quality things—although, I admit I get a bit tired of wearing the same clothes. But, to me, our travel kit is what we need—everything else is what we want. They're optional. When we travel to remote areas of Southeast Asia, South America, or Africa it really sinks in, and we found people have few things—but, they love each other and often look happier than we do. Eating simple foods as well as going for long walks with friends and family can really be a lovely—and, cheap—way to live." He held up his cup. "Refill?"

Paul handed him his cup. "Thanks—it sounds good, but I'm not sure we can live that simply."

"I know—it's certainly different. A year ago, I decided to give away the clothes I hadn't worn in the last year—that turned out to be half of my closet!" He laughed as he recalled

Chapter Three—Homework

the look on Linda's face when he threw an armload of clothes on the dining room table. "Linda thought I finally went completely around the bend! 'You paid a lot of money for those clothes,' she said, and she was right—I spent a fortune on them! But, what's really interesting is what little interest I have in buying clothes now . . ."

Paul accepted the refill, and quickly doctored it with a little cream and sugar. "Although I'm reluctant to talk about the old days, it seems as if people had more self-control over spending. I remember I wanted a portable radio in the worst way. My mother told me I could make it happen, and she helped me look into how I might make the money by having a paper route. Six months later, I had enough in my savings bank . . ." Paul smiled as he remembered the valuable lesson his mom insisted on teaching him. "I actually didn't buy the radio," he continued, "because it was no longer worth it to me—it didn't seem equal in value to all of my hard work. But, I did learn the skill of delayed gratification!"

Dan settled back in his chair. "Meaning?"

"Even at my tender age, it's obvious if people don't have the money for something, they quickly switch to how to finance the purchase."

"True—and, the fact you realize what spending like that can do to a family, you're ahead of the game."

"Today," Paul continued, "it's not uncommon to see students driving nice cars, and going on international vacations. I know tuition is high, but no wonder some of those student loans are six figures!" Both men sat in silence for a moment, considering the state of economic status.

"What's so bad about saying, 'I can't afford it?'"

"You're absolutely right, my friend—there's nothing

wrong with admitting you don't want to spend the money. More people should be like you . . ."

"Right now, it seems pretty easy to be frugal—our incomes are pretty low, and we refuse to have any debt other than our mortgage. And, with Mandy's hospital stay, we don't have money for a big screen TV—the funny thing is when we put off buying anything electronic, it gets cheaper over time."

Dan laughed, raising his coffee mug. "I'll drink to that! Planned obsolescence? Probably. But, you're right—however, once your income starts increasing, you don't want to be in a position of your expenses chasing your income."

Again, silence.

"Here's the thing . . . Dan continued, ". . . try not to lose the message of you don't need all that stuff—if you keep thinking that way, you'll have a bright future."

By the end of the hour, Dan punctuated his logic on expenses by pointing out there are many who are genuinely mystified about where their money is going. And, when you think about it, losing track is easy to do—we don't write many cheques, and bank records are electronic. Why is that important? Because such a lack of paper means we don't have obvious records—no paper trail!

Dan, however, says there is good news—we have great tools. Most people do online banking, and they can view what's going through the charge card at any time, day or night. It's also superb for detecting fraud. Still, to understand what's happening, you might need tools—one of which is Mint. Dan discovered it downloads all online banking and charge card details, but he had to fill in a bunch of information regarding the purchases. A bit time consuming, but certainly faster than recording everything—and, the reports are terrific!

Paul liked the idea of living a more technology-oriented life. He made sure his office technology was up to date, and it made sense he should explore different apps which may make his life easier.

But, introducing Paul to Mint wasn't the last of what Dan had to say that day. He had two more salient points regarding getting expenses under control. The first point? Don't play the 'dumb and dumber game.' By that I mean if the guy gets to have a stag party in Vegas, then the gal gets to also spend money foolishly, as well. Yes, it may sound silly, but couples often get sucked in—the sad thing is you're only hurting your future selves. And, unfortunately, sometimes the dumb and dumber game starts early on in a relationship. For example, consider how elaborate weddings are getting—it's hard to believe everyone can afford them. Yet, they go into debt because of unnecessary expenses when they could have been honest by admitting they couldn't afford it.

The second point? Try to set little milestones. Relish in the delight you feel when you achieve them. Let's say you're paying off a $10,000 student loan at five hundred dollars a month, and you want a three hundred dollar iPad. Try this—get $10,000 in play money, and place it on your fridge as you pay off the loan. The first month the loan is gone, you have an extra five hundred in your pocket. What to do, what to do . . . you could take three hundred, and buy the iPad. If you pay off the loan early, buy the iPad early—just keep the rewards small—nothing like a new car.

By the time Paul headed back to his house, they agreed to discuss big ticket items later in the week. As Paul reached his front door, he was beginning to recognize anything can happen at any time, but there's always a way to protect against it. If he plays it smart!

Chapter Four

Big Ticket Items

"Did you have an opportunity to consider what we talked about at the beginning of the week," Dan asked as he shuffled the cards.

Paul glanced at Mandy. "A little bit—and, by the way, thanks for having us over. Mandy's been itching to do something to get her out of the house!"

Mandy grinned, patting her tummy. "I think this little guy is going to be just like me—he doesn't like staying in the house either!"

"Ahhh . . . a boy, is it? When did you find out?" Linda couldn't disguise her surprise—just last week Mandy said she didn't want to know the gender of her unborn child. 'I want to be surprised,' she said.

"A couple of days ago . . ." She glanced at her friend. "I

know! I know! But, after talking it over with Paul, we figured if we know whether it's a boy or girl, we can target our purchases better—I can't tell you how many of my friends have baby clothes they never use because they're the wrong color!"

Dan burst into a genuine, gut laugh! "Excellent! Good for you! You can plan buying, especially your big ticket items. Cars, for instance..."

Paul grinned. "How is it you know what I'm thinking? We're talking about cars because Mandy's isn't reliable enough..."

"Do you mind," Linda interjected, "if I weigh in on this one?"

"Go for it!"

She fanned the cards in her hand, rearranging according to suit. "I think Dan will agree I was a leader on this—he loves nice cars, and I really don't care. So, I had to push him pretty hard to wait until we were financially comfortable before he had that nice car he always wanted." She glanced up at Paul and Mandy. "We actually drove beaters until our house was paid off!" Then she glanced at her husband. "But, Dan and I were thinking about this, and we don't think you have to go that far. Living right next door, it's tough not to notice what you drive—modest cars."

Paul noticed Mandy rubbing her tummy, and he couldn't help but feel his life was about to change dramatically. He gently held her free hand in his.

"By driving those modest vehicles," Linda continued, "you're likely to save a total of at least six hundred bucks a month in reduced depreciation, interest, and insurance—you may achieve that even net of some increases in maintenance.

Chapter Four—Big Ticket Items

So, Paul, since you're twenty-five, let's say you keep this up for twenty years. At the age of forty-five, you treat yourselves to better cars so this monthly savings no longer happens." She stopped to make sure there weren't glazed-over eyes at the table. "That means," she continued, "at age sixty-five, your fund—at five percent—produces a monthly retirement income of forty-five hundred."

"Your lead," Dan interrupted, nodding to Paul. "She's right—trading in fabulous for modest is a good deal . . ."

Linda played her card, then focused on Paul. "So—when you think of Dan's little visualization of trying to make a fair deal with your future selves—isn't it a fair trade off?"

"Well, when you put it that way . . ." Paul studied his hand for a moment, then played.

"It's kind of weird to think something so simple can make such a difference—and, that's money we can save for the future. The baby . . ." Mandy folded the cards in her hand, grinning at Paul. "I have some ground to make up after that hand!"

Ten minutes later, their first game was in the books. "That's it—girls against the guys! We win!" Linda raised the scorecard in victory.

"I demand a rematch!" Paul looked at his wife. "You up for it? It's still early . . ."

"Yep—but, we kind of got off the subject of the car thing. I'm not sure if I understand completely . . ."

Linda nodded. "I know it sounds crazy—but, driving modest vehicles can produce that kind of long term benefit. I'm sure you noticed my Vibe—it is a basic car, but it meets my needs. I bought it used for about eight thousand, and it's still going strong five years later. Of course, you've seen

Dan's E class Mercedes—brand new, that car was ninety-five thousand. He bought it when it was five years old with one hundred thousand kilometers for twenty-five grand. He doesn't drive much—especially now that he's retired—and, he plans to drive it for approximately five years. When you break it down, his depreciation should be about two hundred and fifty a month while the first owner's was north of one thousand a month." Linda plucked a date and bacon appetizer from her plate. "Of course, I remind him the Vibe's depreciation will only be about one hundred bucks a month, but, I have to admit, his car is a wonderful vehicle for road trips!" She laughed, winking at her husband.

"And, remind me, she does!" Everyone laughed as Mandy dealt the next hand.

As they enjoyed each other's company as well as a spirited card game, Paul realized how comfortable he was with a couple so much older than he and Mandy. If someone would have told him a year ago he would be hanging out with two people on the brink of the geriatric crowd, he would have laughed, saying there was no way. But, as he listened to Dan, he was clear if he listened to what Dan had to say, he and Mandy would be on a pretty darned good road to success.

"I get it—but, it seems to me houses are one of the biggest ticket items I can think of—just for us to buy our house took saving . . ."

"In fact," Mandy commented, "for a time there we almost didn't get it . . ."

"You're right—buying a house is a big commitment." Dan glanced at his wife. "But that doesn't mean it's a good investment—we thought the same thing when we were your age." He checked his watch. "This may take a while—you game?"

Chapter Four—Big Ticket Items

Paul checked with Mandy. "It's up to you . . ."

His wife smiled, and squeezed his hand. "The way I look at it, we're getting information most people pay for—and we're getting it for free! That's what I call a good investment!"

Paul wasn't sure, but he thought Dan blushed at the subtle compliment. "You heard her! We're in . . ."

"Before we get into that, who wants coffee?" Linda grinned at Mandy, "Decaf for you . . ."

Ten minutes later, they were back at the card table, mugs in hand.

"So," Dan began, "When I was a partner at the CPA firm, I used to have little chats with students on personal financial planning—for all of their training in business school, it was amazing what little they knew about this stuff." He paused for a sip. "Anyway—I used to give them a bad time about how most of them drove beautiful new cars when they still hadn't paid off their student loan . . ." He looked over the rim of his cup to quiet stares. "But—I digress. We need to talk about houses . . . most people think houses are great investments, and I simply don't agree."

"I don't get it—it's a big commitment, but you said it isn't a good investment. Why not?" Paul noticed a slight look of concern on his wife's face.

"Well," Dan continued, "over time, they typically go up at the rate of inflation. Now, that's not bad because the gains are tax free—but on a house you own, you'll spend a lot on maintenance and renovations. So—odds are you aren't making that much. In the very long run, the only real value is the land because typically houses get torn down in forty to sixty years." He took a long pause to let his words sink in. "A client spent eighty thousand on a lovely basement renovation three years ago—they just sold their house, and the new owner is tearing it down."

Mandy was stunned. "What? Why on earth would they want to tear it down?"

Dan nodded. "I know—I thought the same thing. But, as you can understand, the eighty grand my client spent on renovations added no value." Another pause. "And, it cost them over two thousand a month . . ."

Paul looked directly at Dan. "What's the solution?"

"Buy small houses, and pay them off. If you move up, try to only do it once or twice in your life—and, keep any new mortgage down to a term of five years."

There was no mistaking the look on Paul's face. "Five years? That's all? How does that work?"

"Simple—just remember the bigger the house, the bigger the property taxes as well as mortgage interest. And, renovations get more expensive because there is more area to renovate."

"What about vacation properties? I talked to a few guys who just bought cabins and, if you ask me, they sure seem expensive . . ."

Dan chuckled, placing his coffee mug on the table. "Funny you should say that—cabins are my pet peeve. Many vacation properties climb in value, but they aren't cheap to run. By owning one, you double up on property taxes, utilities, and repairs. Some of those costs might be lower than the home in town, but what about the cost of a boat?"

"It sounds expensive—I hadn't thought of it that way." Mandy looked at Paul with the 'I'm getting tired' look. "But, do you mind if we take this up another time? I'm ready to call it an evening..."

Dan nodded. "Of course! So, I'll end for the evening by saying this—owning a cabin can be a financial nightmare. But, the main reason cabins are my pet peeve is the dysfunction they often cause in families—it's sad because couples with kids often bought cabins as a source of family fun. Unfortunately, when those kids get married and move away, that cabin ends up being a very significant family asset. Selling it makes everyone mad, but trying to share a cabin between multiple families is extremely challenging. And, if one family is getting the cabin, there may not be enough other assets to keep the other family members happy." Dan sighed, as he got up and pushed in his chair. "It often ends badly—how many parents would buy a cabin if they knew they were increasing the odds of their adult children being estranged?"

"I have a few friends with sad stories like that..." Paul helped Mandy into her coat. "But, I have no intention of setting our children up for something like that..."

"I'm sure you don't," Dan agreed. "Now—get out of here!"

****

By the time Christmas rolled around, Mandy was well on her way to being a great mom. Of course, everyone she knew showered her with baby gifts, but their generosity made Mandy a little uncomfortable. In her mind, some were extravagant, and they reflected a person different than she. After conversations with Dan and Linda, she and Paul were hoping to follow their advice, and extravagance didn't enter into their game plan.

Paul felt the same. Besides, he wanted to make the most use of investments, but he really wasn't sure how to invest or, most important, what he should invest in—the truth was he found the whole investment thing a bit confusing. But, as often is the case, neither Paul nor Dan had the opportunity to talk about investments until after the New Year. Yes, they got together a couple of times for holidays parties at a neighbor's, but that was about it—no time for serious stuff.

It wasn't until Paul's friend approached him with an investment opportunity—one that couldn't miss, according to his friend—they got together. It was right before Valentine's Day Paul had the opportunity to sit down with his neighbor at a new brew pub in town.

After the usual greetings, both men ordered lunch, and settled back. "I really need to talk to you," Paul began. "My brother-in-law has a friend who plays golf with the CFO of a little public oil company—apparently, this oil company might hit it big any day, and the stock could triple." He paused, trying to assess his friend's reaction. "This is really inside information, so it sounds like we can't miss . . ."

Dan eyed the young man. "So, what's keeping you from investing?"

Paul fiddled with the cocktail napkin under his glass. "We really don't have any spare cash lying around because we keep making extra payments on the mortgage whenever we have a bit saved up. But, because our mortgage is in good shape, I think the bank will lend me twenty thousand, or so. " He glanced up. "But, I need to act fast—anyway I'm wondering what you think—who knows? Maybe you'll want a piece of the action!"

Dan took a moment before responding. "Well, Paul,—I can't tell you how many stories like this I've heard in my career. And, I can honestly say it was rare when anything good came of them." He waited for Paul's response. Nothing. "Public stock markets are heavily regulated, and leaking out what is truly inside information is certainly illegal. I, for one, will never get caught up in it."

Paul leveled his eyes on Dan. "So, you think it isn't a good idea . . ."

"Think of it this way—if it works, you could be in trouble. If it doesn't, you'll be kicking yourself for a long time." Dan hesitated. "But, what bothers me most is the family connection—such a high-risk investment just isn't suitable for you. I'm guessing it's not suitable for your brother, either. Is it worth risking the family relationship?"

Paul sat quietly, listening to his friend. "As a young guy," Dan continued, "I was pretty impatient, and made some terrible mistakes. It's like the old joke where the young guy walks into a poker game, and can't figure out who the sucker is. Trust me—you don't want to be that guy . . ."

Paul took a sip, sighing. "I'm sure you're right—I just feel like I want things to happen faster . . ."

Dan laughed. "I know it's pretty boring, but why not stick to paying off your mortgage? You said the interest rate was four percent, right? And, your tax bracket is around thirty-three percent."

Paul nodded.

"So—for you—paying off your non-deductible, 4% mortgage is just as good as finding a totally risk free 6% investment." By the look on Paul's face, Dan could tell he wasn't getting it. He leaned forward. "Here's how it works—say you had $10,000 in your chequing account. If you pay off your mortgage by $10,000 one year later, you reduce your interest expense by $400. Alternatively, say the bank has a one-year GIC at 6%—you make $600, pay taxes of $200, and you are up $400—it's the same thing! But—here's the rub. A one year GIC won't pay 6%—maybe not even 2%. Paying off debt is a terrific investment opportunity, but it's far too little known." Dan paused, looking seriously at Paul. "No one makes money when paying off debt, and that's why it's never advertised . . ."

Paul was lost in thought, thinking about the possibilities.

"If I could find a risk-free investment at 6%," Dan continued, "I would be all over it. Or, 4% risk free and tax free might even suit me better—but, I can't invest in anything like this because it doesn't exist. For you, however, the opportunity is right in front of you. Of course, your situation is pretty good because this is the only loan you have. Imagine all of those poor sods unable to pay off their credit cards every month—what a disaster that is!"

"I suppose if you owe $2,000, and pay 24% a year, you look at the monthly cost of $40, and it doesn't seem like a big deal . . ." Paul's laced his voice with justification.

"I'm sure you're right," Dan agreed. "But, I firmly believe Canadians are far too casual about interest rates—it doesn't matter whether it's the rates they're paying or receiving. In the long run, it's a big deal." He waited, hoping Paul would agree. "Wanna hear something funny? I logged onto the computer the other day, and played around with an example. Say you save $300 a month for forty years—that's a total of $144,000. Then take the fund out equally for the next twenty years . . .

Guess what's the monthly cash flow in retirement? At a

Chapter Four—Big Ticket Items 39

zero interest rate, it's s obviously $600—since you saved for forty years, and withdrew for only twenty years. However, at just 2%, the retirement income almost doubles to $1,115. At 4% it almost doubles again to $2,149. To jump ahead, guess what happens at 10%? The income would be $18,309!"

"But, where . . ."

Dan held up his hand. "I know what you're going to say—where would I earn 10%? Right?"

Paul grinned, and nodded.

"I understand—but lots of people pay rates like that on a loan, especially if their credit rating isn't perfect. And—just for fun—use 24% since people often pay that rate on a credit card. The income in retirement—if you could get 24%—would be over 4 million a month! So, you can see why banks can risk giving young people charge cards." He paused for a drink before continuing. "I understand about 70% of people pay on time, and avoid the interest—but look at the incredible profit that gets made on the other 30%. Anyway, the point is that even with today's low interest rates, most of us are far too casual about rates of return—paying and receiving. I'll feel terrible if somehow your brother in law's tip is great—and legal—and I encouraged you to not get involved. But, truth be told, I would stick to paying off your house. If you're seeking a great return on investment, get ready to own your own plumbing company—I bet you can get that 24% rate of return!"

Chapter Five

First Thoughts on Retirement

At the tail end of late spring, Mandy and Paul brought their new son, Harrison Paul, into the world. They named him in honor of Mandy's grandfather, and the plan was to call him Harry—yes, the name was a bit old-fashioned, but the young couple was determined to keep all aspects of their lives simple and unencumbered. 'Harry' seemed a strong name and, if he were anything like Mandy's grandfather—well, success was sure to be in the cards for their boy.

As you may guess, having a child changed their lives more than they imagined, and Paul found himself thinking about years down the road—many years. Retirement. Considering retirement in his twenties was something the majority of their friends didn't do, but Paul was beginning to feel the weight of their new responsibility. Clearly, he needed to make certain their son had a good start in life—

but, he also needed to consider what life would be like when that brand spankin' new baby graduated from college, and headed off on a life of his own.

Over the course of previous months, Paul and Dan had little time to get together. Dan and Linda's daughter moved back to her hometown, and they were spending time getting her settled—plus the occasional babysitting gig when she needed it. Paul didn't hear him in the backyard as much as he did in the fall, and it was no secret he missed his neighbor's guidance. So, it was a perfect day when Paul heard a lawnmower cough to life in his neighbor's yard—maybe he could get Dan's opinion about registered retirement savings plans.

He waited for the mower to sputter, then conk out. "Hey, neighbor! Need some help?"

"If you're a lawnmower mechanic, yes—if not, I can still use the moral support!"

"Hang on—I'll be right over! I'll come through the back gate . . ."

"Roger that . . . I appreciate it!"

A few minutes later, Paul and Dan were studying the lawnmower. After a few attempts at unsuccessful starts, Paul determined either the air filter was clogged, or there was a fouled plug.

"If it's the plug," Paul suggested, "All you have to do is take it out to clean it—if it's the air filter, buy a new one. It's a cheap fix . . ."

"I've had this thing for years," Dan confessed. "Maybe it's time to retire it, and get a new one . . ."

Paul looked at him with surprise. "Doesn't that go

Chapter Five—First Thoughts on Retirement

against your strategy about saving money?" He laughed, as he checked the gas. "And, speaking of retirement—I've been looking at RRSPs."

"Really? You're thinking about retirement? I guess bringing Harry into the world changes your perspective a bit, eh?"

"It does—but, to be honest, I'm not sure what I need, and there are a bunch of plans. I'm amazed by how many ads there are for RRSPs—and, most of them make it sound like I can retire somewhat young, and loaded." Paul folded a paper towel in quarters as he prepared to check the oil in the mower.

"That's for sure and, to be honest, I have mixed feelings about them. So, the shortest answer I can give you is the right RRSP depends on your personal situation . . ."

"Okay—I get that. But, you've known us for a while, so what do you think we should consider?"

Dan took a seat on the low, brick garden wall, placing the cap back on the two gallon gas can. "Well—the government created them back in 1957. At that time, a lot of people would work for one company most of their lives, and many had pretty good pension plans. But, if you didn't have a pension, there was no tax incentive to save for retirement." He paused to take gulp of water. "Around that time, Canada was bringing in social programs—the government knew if people became poor seniors, there would be a huge pressure on these programs."

Paul couldn't help but look confused. "I was told seniors don't get welfare—is that true?"

"Not really. In addition to Old Age Security, if a senior's income is low enough, they get a supplement—even if they own a lot of assets. So, the supplement is easier to qualify for than welfare." Dan stopped, looking at his friend. "Have I lost you?"

Paul chuckled. "Not yet!"

"So," Dan continued, "it's in the government's interest to encourage people to support themselves when they get old. With RRSPs, the idea is a portion of your income can go into a before tax savings program. In fact, RRSPs are often called the pension program for people without a pension..."

"If I have a pension, I can't have a RRSP?"

"You might be able to have a smaller RRSP—are you clear on how it works?"

Paul shook his head. "Not really..."

"Okay. This is how it works—say you make $100,000, and you do have a pension. Let's say you put in $5,000 a year, and your employer matches it—that's $10,000 going into the plan. Now, to see if you can also put some to an RRSP, we need to know your total limit. The RRSP limit is 18% or—with an income of $100,000—that equals $18,000. But, since $10,000 went into the pension, your RRSP limit reduces by $8,000." He looked again at his young neighbor. "Are you with me?"

"Yep—so far!"

"Excellent! I know these things can be tricky—so, if there's something you don't understand, just stop me..."

Paul nodded.

"So," Dan continued, "the total going into both plans is still $18,000. Once in a while, I saw someone who couldn't contribute, at all—but, normally, the RRSP limit is just reduced by the total pension contributions. The rules in this area are pretty complicated, but they only affect the small number of Canadians who have pensions.

"Are pensions and RRSPs taxed the same?"

"Ah! Excellent question! Generally—yes. Taxes are paid only when you take out the money—and, you don't need to keep track of what portion of money is original savings or what part is investment income. Nothing has been taxed yet, so the entire withdrawal is income."

"But, how can it be that simple? I thought if I buy a stock and it goes up, the profit was only half taxable. And, if I lose money on the stock, aren't there restrictions?"

"You're right—the losses are only one half deductible, and only against capital gains. But—here's the thing. With RRSPs and pensions, it's brutally simple—everything that comes out is fully taxed. That means capital gains become fully taxable—but, on the flip side, I guess you can also say losses are fully deductible. Since the plan fell in value, there is less to take out and, therefore, less income."

Paul topped off the oil in the mower, then wiped his hands and sat next to Dan. "The other day at the bank, there was a poster for one of their mutual funds—a 'dividend fund' they called it. I'm guessing the fund owns shares that pay dividends." He paused to think for a moment. "So, what are they, and how are they taxed?"

"Another good question—when a company has a profit, generally, the company pays taxes. Some companies don't need all the money they make, so they hand it out to the shareholders—those handouts are dividends. For example, let's say your share of the company pre-tax profit is $10,000. The company pays a tax of about 25%, so the $10,000 drops down to $7,500.

In Canada, we have a smart system—the law says your personal taxes on dividends should be lower since the company already paid tax. So, say you make around $60,000, and your marginal tax rate is 32%. That means if you made another $10,000 of normal income, the tax on it would be $3,200."

Just as Dan was to complete the example, Paul's cell buzzed. Paul checked, closing the screen before returning it to his pocket. "That was Mandy—she's wondering what's taking so long!"

"Everything okay?"

"She's fine, thanks—I said I'd be just a little longer . . ."

"Okay . . . where was I? Ah, yes! So—using our example—we said your share of the company profit was $10,000, and the company tax on it was $2,500. So, isn't it logical the personal tax on your dividend of $7,500, should only be $700?" He glanced at Paul. "The total tax is still $3,200—that's just adding the tax of $2,500 the company paid, plus the tax you paid on the dividend of $700."

"Seems fair to me . . ."

"I agree—but, if that dividend went to your RRSP, it gets taxed the same as employment or interest income. True, it's wonderful the personal tax is delayed until you take it out. But—if you're still in the 32% bracket—the tax will be $3,200 instead of $700.

Paul thought about Dan's example for several moments. "So, let me see if I have this right—the RRSP ads I see are pushing me to invest in the stock market. If what I make are capital gains and dividends, isn't it a really bad idea? Won't I pay way more tax than I should?"

"Indeed. But, you're paying the tax decades later—

maybe. It works really well in terms of compounding all of your profits without paying immediate tax. But, when you pay, you really pay—ask any senior about the tax they're paying on their RRSP, and most of them are pretty angry about it. The sad thing is most people assume they'll pay less tax when they're a senior—when I was in practise, I did thousands of personal tax returns, and I would say it's almost never true. Seniors pay more . . ."

"But what about seniors with very low income? Surely many must be paying nothing . . ."

"Well—it depends what you call tax. Typically, if a senior isn't paying tax, they're collecting the Old Age Security Supplement as I mentioned before. So, it is kind of a negative income tax—when your income goes up even a little bit, this supplement is usually cut by 50%. That means when seniors with a very low income collect a small RRSP, although they don't pay tax, they see a 50% drop in supplement. When I prepared tax returns for poor seniors, explaining what the RRSP did to them was a pretty tough conversation—because their income was low when they were working, they only saved around 25% when they bought the RRSP. They thought that was a good deal because they figured they wouldn't pay tax once they retired." Dan paused, shaking his head. "Seeing the supplement drop by 50% is quite a shock! That's a worse "tax" rate than NHL hockey players pay. . . ."

"It seems as if the Canadian system can be pretty heartless," Paul commented with a tone of disgust.

"Heartless, indeed—and, the problem isn't just OAS supplement. There are various other tax and other types of benefits seniors can enjoy, and those benefits get taken away quickly as income rises—the wealthier seniors can get their basic Old Age Security taken away completely."

Paul glanced at his watch. "I better be getting back—so,

what's the take-away?"

"The bottom line is almost no seniors are happy about collecting RRSPs..."

"So, if they're wealthy, why don't they just leave the plan untouched?"

"They can't—they have to start taking it out the year they turn seventy-one." Dan paused. "Have you heard the term 'RRIF'?

Paul shook his head.

"That's an RRSP converted to something that pays you—and, you can't put money in anymore, either."

"Okay—so why not take out very little?"

"You can't do that either, unfortunately—there's a minimum percentage you have to take. In your seventies, it's around 8%. If the investments are earning—say... 10%—it means your RRIF can still be growing. But, in your eighties, the percentage you take out rises to about 10%. If you get to your mid-nineties, you'll be forced to take out 20% a year."

"So—what happens when I die? There's probably something left, right? What happens then?"

"Well—with both pensions and RRSPs—if you leave it to your spouse, it's sort of like nothing happens. The rules on pensions are variable and complex. There may or may not be a continuing benefit to your surviving spouse. Sometimes, that depends on choices you make—normally, on pensions, the value falls to nothing once you and your spouse die. With RRSPs, your spouse just takes over the plan. However, if you don't have a spouse—or didn't leave the RRSP to her—whatever is left in the plan is taxed as income in your last personal tax return. So, your kids gets what's left after the tax is paid..."

Paul leveled a long look at his friend. "So, are you saying the kids hoping to inherit are better off if their parents have a RRSP instead of a pension?"

"I suppose the simple answer is you're right—but, I guess it depends on how big the RRSP is. Having no pension and a RRSP under $400,000 likely means the RRSP will run out, and the kids will be supporting the parents one day. Of course, it depends on the parents' spending, how the RRSP is invested, and how long the parents live." A pause. "So—I say good pensions get high marks for taking care of seniors while they're alive. The kids will not inherit the pension—but, at least the kids don't need to support their parents."

Paul stood, extending his hand. "Good advice, as always! Give my best to Linda—I gotta get my butt home!"

****

Around midsummer, Paul decided it was time to spruce up his front yard. He took a serious look at the flower beds lining the driveway, arriving at the decision it was time to take a stand. With Mandy busy as a mom, asking Dan to help him seemed the best solution. As he assessed the work, it was clearly a two-man job.

Two days later, both men stood at the driveway's edge, a

cooler filled with water and sodas in the shade by the garage door.

Paul glanced at Dan. "How about I take the left, and you take the right. Mandy wants us to alternate a bush with a group of flowers . . ."

Dan eyed his friend. "I take it she didn't trust your design sense . . ."

Paul laughed, jamming the spade into the ground. "For that, I suggest a friendly bet—you win, I take you to lunch. I win—the other way around. Whoever makes it to the end of their side of the driveway first . . ."

Dan let out a belly laugh. "You're on!"

An hour later, both men reached the end of the driveway at the same time. "Draw?" Dan asked, laughing.

Paul agreed. "I'm ready to call it a day—name your poison. Water or soda?"

"Water, please . . ."

Paul grabbed two waters from the cooler, then pulled up a chair on the broad front porch—as far as Paul was concerned, the veranda was what he liked best about the house. Mandy enjoyed sitting there in her favorite rocker, Harry asleep on her chest. For Paul? Well, it reminded him of when he was a kid. His grandparents had a farm just outside of town, and the main house had a porch that wrapped around three sides. Even on the hottest summer nights there was a cooling breeze, and Paul recalled the sense of calm he felt every time he visited.

"I appreciate the help—I promise I won't ask you to help with the backyard!" Paul held his water bottle up in a mock toast.

Chapter Five—First Thoughts on Retirement

"Not a problem—glad to help." Dan returned the toast, then paused for a moment, enjoying the cool sip of water. "So—what did you decide to do about the RRSP?"

Paul swiped at his mouth as couple drips of water made it onto his chin. "We didn't—I need to have a better understanding before we jump into it . . ."

"How so?"

"Well, I guess I don't know what you think about RRSPs for Mandy and me—I do hope to own my own plumbing company one day. Plumbing company owners—generally—seem to make a lot more than plumbers who work for them. So, I'm working on what I need to know by starting to do estimating—and, I love the commercial jobs. But, if I started my own company, I'll need some money behind me. Paying off the house is going well, but it's going to take a while—although, I could do some saving over and above that. If I bought RRSPs with those savings, wouldn't my savings be that much bigger because I could throw in the taxes I would save? What do you think?"

"I like that you're thinking about different possibilities—but, there's a problem with that scenario. RRSPs can only invest in qualified investments—most common, GIC's and publically traded stocks and bonds. What you can't do is have your RRSP lend the money to a private company you and Mandy own . . ."

Paul drained the last bit of water from the bottle. "Really? That doesn't seem too bright to me—doesn't the government want to encourage small businesses to start up, hire people, and grow?"

Dan sighed. "Well, they do, but what you laid out just isn't the kind of 'support' the government offers—there's a great tax deferral program once you get your company up and operating. It's one of the best tax deferral programs in the world. But, for now, I suggest you keep that money for starting a business, and stay away from RRSPs."

"I understand it—kind of. I do much better if I can see exactly what you're talking about . . ."

"Come with me!" Dan's knees creaked as he rose. "I can show you—let's head back to my house . . ."

"What for?" Paul figured Dan had information already laid out—something he could take with him.

"Computer—I think once you see the numbers, you'll understand it . . ."

"Lead the way!"

A few minutes later, both men were sitting in front of Dan's desktop computer.

"So . . ." Dan scrolled down to the second page. "We'll compare saving up for your business with and without using an RRSP. Let's assume you saved—outside an RRSP—at $7,000 per year for five years for a total of $35,000. Let's also say you can invest the funds at 3%, and we'll use 2% for the after- tax rate. Then, we'll look at the ultimate growth for those same investments if you used an RRSP, cashing it all in after the five years . . ."

Paul studied the numbers—but, if he had to be honest, some of it was confusing. However, as long as he could learn little by little, he felt confident he would create the perfect financial plan for his family. "Okay—so far, so good . . ."

"Good—so, saving $7,000 a year with a 2% return, it grows to $36,818, after tax. Of course, the income is less than $2,000—but, it's only five years and the interest rate is small. Now let's consider RRSPs—right now, you're in the 32%

bracket, so the tax saving will be $2,240. Add that to your savings of $7,000, and it jumps to $9,240 or $770/month." He glanced at Paul. "Still making sense?"

Paul nodded.

"Good—now, we use the full 3% investment rate since there is no short-term tax. Look here . . ." Dan pointed the cursor on numbers in the third column. "The computer says that works out to $49,909 . . ."

"Holy cow! That's a major difference! If I follow that plan, I'm miles ahead!"

Dan held up his hand. "Hold on—to get it into your company's account, you have to cash it in. So, let's assume when you cash this in, your salary is $20,000 higher—then you have to add the $49,909 from the RRSP to that higher income."

Paul looked as if the light came on. "I'm guessing that means a high tax . . ."

"Bingo! Look here . . ." Again, Dan placed the cursor on a specific number. "The computer is telling me the tax on the RRSP is $17,452—that means you'll only have $32,457 left."

"What? That's crazy! Going that route, I'll lose almost $4,400—I'll be better off hiding the money in my mattress!"

Dan laughed. "You might be right! And, I haven't told you the other bad news—when you bought that $7,000 a year for five years then cashed it in, your right to buy RRSPs in future is permanently lowered by $35,000. Cashing it in doesn't restore your right to make that purchase. Why, I don't know—it doesn't make sense to me, but rules are rules."

"So . . ." Paul hesitated as he tried to work through something in his mind. "Are they ever a good deal?"

"I think so—RRSPs work well for people with steady jobs who consistently save until retirement. But, it's a terrible plan for saving up to start a business..."

Paul sat back in his chair, focusing on the computer screen. "There's something else—we've been talking like I'm not in a pension, but I am. CPP comes off my cheque, and my boss tells me he has to match what I put in... how does that compare?"

"Interesting question—Canadian Pension Plan is a strange, fifty-year-old government program. Originally, contributions were much too low, and CPP was on the verge of failure twenty years ago. But, the program was saved in 1997, and now it's a bad deal—but it will survive, unlike similar programs in other countries.

"Why is it a bad deal?"

"Well, let's say I was selling it to you as an investment. At twenty-five, you work for forty years and, at age sixty-five, you take it out and get maximum benefits for twenty years before dying at age eighty-five." Dan scrolled down another page. "Here's the return—the maximum employee contribution is $202 a month, and the maximum benefit is $1,038 a month. Yes, that's over five times what you put in—but, remember you only collect for twenty years and you contributed for forty." Dan took a second to find the number indicating rate of return. "Check it out—that's a return rate of 3%."

Paul nodded. "I get it—but, I have to tell you that doesn't sound too bad to me. Interest rates are lower than that..."

"True—but haven't we forgotten something?"

Paul thought for a second, then grinned at his friend. "Of course! What happened to the money my boss put in?"

"Exactly! Let's put in your contributions and his—that doubles the contribution to $404/month. See? The interest rate now drops to 0.824% . . ."

Paul was quiet as he considered Dan's information.

"And, remember," Dan continued, "rates are at historical lows. Long term investments like a pension should really do a lot better than under 1%. At higher rates of return, benefits goes up. At 5%, the monthly benefit is over $4,000 per month—at 10%, it's over $24,000 a month." Dan paused, thinking about CPP. "You can see the CPP is far from a good plan—it can't compete in the open market. It exists only because the government forces it on us. Sure—for some people it's great because if they have free choice, they would save nothing for retirement. For the rest of us, in my opinion, it's awful." He shifted in his chair, and looked at Paul. "But, I haven't told you the worst part of the plan . . ."

"Oh, swell—I'm depressed enough already!"

"Sorry, mate—but think about this. Let's say we go back to using a low rate like 3%, and see what the computer says." He focused on the computer screen. "See here? At age sixty-five, the pension you and your boss paid for should be worth about $375,000. Guess what happens if you and Mandy died in a car accident at sixty-five? Your death benefit is $2,500 each—the rest of the money is just gone . . ."

Paul stared at the screen. "Wow—I thought calling it awful was over the top. What can I do?"

"Employees have no option—but, once you start your own company, you and Mandy can live off dividends. Since you aren't getting a salary, you don't contribute to CPP."

"Sounds good, but what's the catch?"

"The hardest part is having the discipline to save money

for retirement some other way . . . luckily, you and Mandy are pretty frugal. However, for business owners who spend foolishly, staying with salary means their retirement income is CPP—at a minimum."

Paul looked at Dan, a smile taking root. "My head hurts," he laughed. "I never thought I'd say this, but let's power through the last row of plants . . . I need something to take my mind off this!"

"You're on!"

Chapter Six

Retirement Plan for Employees

It hardly seemed a year since Paul and Mandy moved into their new home. Mandy loved being a mom, but she discovered it may be more difficult than she thought to balance a home business with raising a family. It was tough—but, she never thought for one second she wasn't up to the challenge.

Paul, on the other hand, was tackling his plumbing education with gusto and, after hearing a few of the guys talking at work about employee retirement plans, he figured it was something he should know. After all, the harder he worked, the more he knew he would start his own business. And, as a business owner, it was on him to know as much as he could about all things employees. But, he was an employee himself, and he needed to take that into consideration.

Since the gardening episode, Paul and Dan had little

time to get together—again. Harry was a healthy little boy, and Paul relished spending every spare moment with him and Mandy. When he really thought about it, life before Harry seemed so simple—it wasn't, but comparisons often involve seeing things differently. His stress level spiked every once in a while, but he managed to keep life in perspective. And, the best way to do that? Learn. Paul needed to learn as much as he could—and, what he needed was information on employee retirement plans. Up until then, he was trying to think like a business owner. But, the truth was opening his own business was at least a couple of years down the road. It didn't make sense to him he should wait to begin a retirement savings plan—two years of doing nothing? That didn't make sense, at all!

He had to wait, however—Dan and Linda were on an extended trip, so that left him to his own devices. Research left him wanting to know more, so he bit the bullet and emailed his friend with his question.

Hey, Dan!

Hope you're having the time of your life! Mandy and I are keeping an eye on things, so you can continue your vacation without worry!

So, I'm sorry to ask you this, but I have a question that's driving me nuts! Don't feel as if you have to respond—I can certainly wait for your answer. If, however, you feel like spending quality time with your laptop, I'll appreciate hearing from you!

Here's the deal—I've been listening to guys at work about how they expect to retire. A lot of them sound pretty positive, but what I'm hearing is if I work hard and pay my maximum RRSP, I'll be fine. But, in the paper the other day, an article said most Canadians are in for a shock—unless they inherit or win the Loto, they're going to need to dramatically cut their expenses in retirement...

Like I said, this can wait until you get back...

Have fun!

****

Two days later, Paul's cell notified him of a new email—it was Dan.

Hey!

I laughed when I read your email—I wish all of my 'students' took what I tell them as seriously as you!

First things first—we're having a great time and, as I write this Linda is in town, window shopping. So, it seems a good time to answer your question...

I know you and Mandy are frugal, liking to stick to a plan. But appreciate—statistically—few Canadians are like the two of you. Their houses are too big, they don't put away maximum RRSP contributions, and they spend way too much in relation to their income. So, your own situation doesn't look too bad—but it's all about financial discipline. In other words, don't tell your buddies at work they will be okay!

For you, I assumed your family income was roughly $100,000, and it will stay about the same until you semi-retire at fifty-five. I also assumed you will work enough part-time *from fifty-five to sixty-five to pay your bills. By that I mean you won't be adding to or taking from the retirement fund. At sixty-five, I assumed full retirement as well as the both of you will live to eighty-five. Most important, from now until age fifty-five, you put the maximum 18% into your RRSPs.*

That last assumption is pretty tough for most couples—after you pay your taxes—CPP, EI, mortgage payment, and $18,000 contribution to RRSP—you and Mandy will only be able to spend about $5,000 per month. Of course, when your house is paid off you'll have a bit more elbow room—but that's twenty years away. Even so, you can see how most couples can't pull this off with expensive cars and elaborate vacations.

Another critical assumption is what kind of returns you get in your RRSP—I assumed you'll beat inflation by 2%. That can be very tough to do, but it's possible . . . anyway, my calculations have you and Mandy being able to spend about $5,600/month in retirement.

Let's talk when we return in three weeks—hi to Mandy for us!

Three weeks was perfect—it gave Paul time to write down the questions he would have based on Dan's assumptions. With projections for retirement, having over five grand to spend a month was a number with which he could work.

He was pretty sure Mandy would like the number, too!

****

Chapter Six—Retirement Plans for Employees

True to his word, Paul's neighbors returned by late August, and he and Dan made plans to attend one of the local high school ball games. Faint signs of summer's fading were beginning to appear, and there was a crispness in the night air as they sat in the school's bleachers.

Paul attended the high school several years earlier, and he was known as being one of the best young athletes within the last decade. Many thought he may pursue sports as a career, but doing so didn't really interest him—he was more of a hands-on kind of guy. Besides, going into sports wouldn't do much for his future, and he figured being an entrepreneur business owner was more suited to his style. And, he told Dan so as they watched his old team fight for victory.

"So—did you have a chance to write down questions about employee retirement plans," Dan asked.

"Yep—the first thing I want to know about is Old Age Security. We'll get that on top of everything else—right?"

Dan looked at him. "No—I included your Old Age Securities, and that may be optimistic. The government is weakening or eliminating that program as time goes on—they already considered delaying the starting age to sixty-seven. Phased in over time, yes, but it would certainly have applied to couples your age, and who knows what changes are coming?"

Paul was quiet, thinking about the numbers.

"So," Dan continued, "if there were no OAS, your spending will have to be more like $4,500 a month. Basically, that's just your RRSP income, plus what you'll get from CPP—less the income taxes, of course. As we discussed, the maximum CPP is just over $1,000 a month, and you'll likely get less if you cut back to part time for ten years. I assumed about $800/month..."

"On the RRSP, that's just the income—is that right? In other words, the big pot of savings is still there..."

"No—sorry. I have you spending the investment income and the principle, so the RRSP runs out when you're eighty-five."

"But, what if we live longer? Or, it costs us more to live?"

"Well, I guess it shows how tight this plan is—there isn't a lot of room for error. I know it sounds crazy, but a big problem is outliving your retirement fund..."

"Then there's inflation—did you take that into account?"

"Sort of—I factored it in by limiting the RRSP investment rate to 2%, assuming inflation eats up the rest. Also, CPP benefits rise slowly—but, overall, you're right to be concerned. More Canadians should be—just putting in the maximum RRSP is a plan that has little elbow room for any false steps. Of course, as the paper said, something like a big inheritance would really help."

Paul laughed. "I doubt Mandy and I are likely to inherit very much—both of us come from big families! Frankly, I'm worried we may have to support our parents because of the issues you mentioned." He paused. If they became responsible for the well-being of their parents, that changed the picture considerably. "So—if you were me, what would you do to give yourself some more room for error? Our house is modest, we don't drive fancy cars, and we keep our spending right down to what feels pretty tight. Frankly, in retirement we dream of owning a sailboat—like you—or traveling around the world. Maybe both..."

"Let's think back to our earlier chat on financial planning—the key issues were income, living expenses, big ticket items, and investing your retirement funds. As you just said, the spending and big ticket items are well controlled . . ."

"And," Paul interjected, "I remember you talked about high-risk investing such as a hot tip on the stock market not working too well." He paused, working through their last several conversations. "I guess it comes down to income, doesn't it?"

"Yep—you got it. I can't see any other way to build some elbow room into your financial plan. I guess—in the short run—you can take all the overtime you can stand, or do little plumbing jobs for people after hours. Plus, Mandy can help in whatever way she can—believe me, being a mom is going to keep her busy. But, I keep coming back to the idea of the two of you owning your own company—a conversation for another time . . ."

Paul nodded. "Agreed—the game is getting good!"

****

The bottom line was Paul wanted to own his own plumbing company, and there were things he could do to make that dream a reality. He was already taking steps—he was promoted to Head Crew Chief at work, so he ran the bigger, tougher jobs. He was also sitting in with his boss to learn estimating and, not only that, Nick's bookkeeper was slated to retire soon. That tidbit of information inspired Mandy to sign up for a few night courses to improve her skills with cost accounting in order to calculate how much profit was earned on each job. Taking classes certainly couldn't hurt—his boss's accounting procedures were downright basic and, if Mandy had the opportunity to apply newer, more effective procedures, well, it could help when they were ready to open their own business.

When he told Dan about their progress, Dan was impressed they were taking their future seriously—but, there was more they could do such as talking to owners of plumbing companies. Dan was a firm believer in picking their brains—learn why they think they're successful, as well as their biggest challenges. Not only that, he could also talk to general contractors—they would certainly know what they like and don't like about plumbing companies.

The fact is, he thought, *I can't do too much research. Men especially tend to throw caution to the wind, and just go for it—maybe that's why men fail in business more than women.* He learned that from Dan—and, Paul loved the idea of Mandy's being the future bookkeeper of his boss's company. He figured couples having roles in their family businesses tended to do well—it also seemed part of the problem was almost no one is good at every role a successful business needs.

Even though Paul didn't read as much as Mandy would have liked, Dan lent him his copy of *The E-myth Revisited* by Michael Gerber. According to Dan, Gerber does a great job of describing the very dilemma Paul and Mandy were facing. Dan wanted Paul to learn that he and Mandy, together, would be a stronger management team based on the fact they have different strengths and weaknesses. And that should be their main consideration . . .

Chapter Six—Retirement Plans for Employees

Why businesses succeed or fail.

Paul asked Dan about the hundreds of businesses he saw during his estate planning years—did he ever figure out why some businesses make it while others fail?

He did.

They discussed it when Paul was babysitting Harry, and Dan stopped by to return the drill he borrowed.

"You know the old saying about real estate—location, location, location. For small businesses, I think the big three are management, management, and management," he said, thinking for a moment about how he should frame their discussion. "Successful business owners share some common traits—first, they have a passion for what they're doing. Typically, they're on a mission to fill a need, or simply be the best at what their business does—they don't give up when setbacks occur."

Paul nodded. "Giving up isn't an option—at least it isn't with me . . ."

Dan smiled at his friend. "An admirable trait, Paul, to be sure . . ." He paused. "Instead, they patiently keep positive, determined to get back on track with the mission. If you simply want to forget about work when it's five o'clock, or only go into the business because you think you'll make a pile of money, it's probably best to remain an employee . . ."

"Why do you say that?"

"Well, let me ask you—is every boss you had a good boss?"

Paul chuckled at the question. "Funny you ask—when you described good business owners, I was thinking of Bob's Plumbing because Bob was my first boss. He was dismal in almost every area you mentioned." He paused. "Plus, he was a jerk. I couldn't trust him, and his customers were often pissed off at him. I guess you get what you pay for—they only chose his business because he was the cheapest. He would tear a strip of you if anything went wrong long before he got the story straight." Paul glanced at Dan. "The only good thing about Bob was since his employees were always quitting, I could get hired on as a new apprentice. Most of the plumbing shops only wanted experienced employees..."

"What about your current boss?"

"Oh, man—working for Nick is terrific! He's a pleaser—he wants customers to be happy with what we did so they'll tell their friends about him." Paul grinned as he described Nick. "General contractors will hire him even though his prices aren't the lowest, but they know he'll do what he said he would do—and, he'll do it right. He's fair with employees, but if a new guy comes in and doesn't share Nick's passion for doing things right and treating customers like kings, Nick will run him off pretty fast. He seems to read people pretty quickly—if someone fools him, it isn't for long. And, I have to admit, it's a big reason I work there. I want to be proud of what I do, and proud of the company..."

"Do you speak up when you see something going wrong?"

"Yep—I try to act like Nick is my partner. That way, I can learn more about the business, and make Nick's life a bit easier, too. He's a great guy—I'd do whatever he asked me to do, and more..."

"Nice! So, from your experience, you recognize a great business owner and leader. But, you can also learn a lot from the Bobs of the world..."

"True—but, guys with good attitudes can also fail..."

Dan shrugged, recalling several business men who failed in spite of their positive attitudes. "Sadly, yes. But, to be fair, sometimes it can be bad luck—starting a business when the economy goes into a big downturn can knock out even the best guys. More often, the basic reason is they're undercapitalized—they just didn't have enough money behind them. Or, they try to grow too quick—and, one of the biggest mistakes is trying to bite off too much."

"What do you mean? Give me an example . . ."

Dan thought for a moment. "Sure—a guy came in many years ago, and he was going to do a whole new kind of wallpaper where the pattern didn't repeat. He spent all of his money perfecting this idea. Then he went to the guys who print wallpaper, and they were working flat out printing the old style wallpaper . . ."

Paul looked at Dan, confused. "Not sure I get it . . ."

"In other words," Dan continued, "his was a solution to a problem that didn't exist. Wallpaper was selling like crazy! His customer wasn't the home owner—it was the people who print wallpaper."

"Shouldn't he have figured that out beforehand?"

"Of course! What it points out, however, is the lack of a business plan—there are all kinds of good sources on what should go into a business plan. Unfortunately, people don't do any of the work because they're in love with an idea—they really don't want to find out there are real problems with it."

Paul grew quiet, thinking about how a business plan will benefit him when the time comes for him to go off on his own. To build his business.

To be successful on his own.

Chapter Seven

Cash Flow vs. Profit

Dan waded in several inches of water as it flooded his basement at an alarming rate. He bailed, while Linda dialed Paul's number, filling him in on the crisis.

Five minutes later, Paul stood in his neighbor's basement—only moments went by before he diagnosed the problem. "Well, that old hot water heater was going to go eventually—turns out today was the day. I can pick one up tomorrow for about half of what you would pay and install it tomorrow evening . . ."

"Excellent! Of course, I'll reimburse you—but surely that's not enough . . ."

Paul shot a large grin at his friend. "Please—you gave me a lot of terrific advice—this is my chance to return the favor . . ."

"Much appreciated . . ." Dan shook Paul's hand as he

walked him to the door.

"Of course," Paul reminded him, "you won't have hot water until tomorrow night—you're going to have to rough it!"

"No problem—I'll be home after four o'clock tomorrow afternoon. Any time after that is great . . ."

****

"I'm amazed at how fast you can do that! Will I notice any changes?" Dan stood in front of his new hot water heater, hands in his pockets.

"Well—your gas bill might drop a bit. That old tank you had was pretty inefficient . . ."

"That'll be nice!" He looked directly at Paul. "Which reminds me—have you had a chance to look at business plans yet?"

Paul laughed. "You know I did! And, you probably know I have a few questions . . ."

"Such as?"

"I'm not sure I really understand cash flow—and, how it relates to profit. I mean, I get the basics, but, from what I

Chapter Seven—Cash Flow vs. Profit

read, there's a lot more to it . . .

"I get it—but it's important you understand it completely. On the income side—when you bill someone—you have an immediate revenue. However, they might take months to pay you. In construction, for example, it can be a lot worse because general contractors often drag out their payments to you as long as they can. And, of course, there is the holdback."

"Holdback?"

Dan nodded. "By law, customers are allowed to not pay a percentage of the final bill for a while—on the expense side, employees will quit if they aren't paid every payday. I assure you, suppliers of material aren't keen on giving credit . . ."

"I'll say! At my work, almost all of them want us to pay in ten days—they cut their invoices by 2% as an incentive, and we always take them up on that offer."

"Another thing your boss is doing right!" Dan paused to collect his thoughts. "Okay, so let's say you have a job you bid at $100,000. The labor cost is $30,000, and the material is $50,000—so, you're expecting a profit of $20,000." Dan motioned for Paul to join him at the kitchen table.

"And, we'll be paying out the entire labor bill immediately. Even if we get 2% off on the material, that's still paying out $49,000 before we bill the $100,000, let alone collect it. So the bank is down $79,000. But that's just temporary—surely everyone can see that . . ."

"I wish that were true—the problem is your suppliers and the bank have no idea whether you'll be successful. For new businesses, suppliers will be reluctant to grant you much credit—and the days of the friendly understanding bank manager are over. Do you know banks largely use computers to make leading decisions? Until you're well established, borrowing against receivables is almost impossible. In the old days, you would likely get a phone call before the banks would bounce cheques. Now? It happens automatically . . ."

"Couldn't I sell the receivables?"

"It's possible—the technical term is 'factoring.' But, the problem with construction is the customer has the right to not pay if the work isn't done properly. Because that's a judgment call, the factoring company doesn't want to be caught in the middle. So it's unlikely you can sell or 'factor' the receivables." Dan hesitated to make certain he wasn't piling too much on his young friend. "Plus," he continued, "factoring isn't cheap—you may lose a big chunk of your profit."

Paul chewed on Dan's comment about the existing possibility of losing a good chunk of change. It was becoming increasingly clear he was going to need a sizable sum to get his plumbing business up and running—just to be on the safe side.

"It seems cash flow is a big problem—I see I'll need a couple of hundred grand to get my business going. Tools. Down payments on things such as trucks and forklifts. Things I might not count on—but, the big thing is the receivables could explode . . ."

"You're exactly right—you must have noticed some companies stay small, asking their customers to pay for materials up front as well as asking for payments on labor very regularly . . ."

"Oh, yeah—those little guys are out there but, typically, they can only do little repair jobs like your water heater. There's competition in that market, and there are hidden costs." Paul glanced at Dan. "I'm sure you already know this, but homeowners often want estimates—even on tiny jobs! I don't blame them, really, but estimates take a lot of time—it's no wonder it's tough to get ahead, and the work isn't exactly charming, either." It didn't take a genius to realize commercial jobs were more lucrative.

Dan explained how many new restaurants go through the same thing—they survive for about six months based cash flow.

"Think about it for a sec—the restaurant collects immediately..."

"True," Paul agreed, "but wouldn't their employees and suppliers want quick payment?"

"That's right—but collections still run ahead of most payments. Even a few weeks gives them a cash flow advantage—but there is another 'supplier' we haven't talked about, and they get stiffed all the time..."

Paul thought about which supplier that could be, but finally gave up. "Who's that?"

"The government—the restaurant collects GST from customers. Of course, the restaurant will pay out some GST as well, but only on things like rent and booze. There is no GST on basic food items—and, of course, no GST is charged by employees. The idea is GST is not supposed to be a tax on businesses—the business simply collects and pays it."

"But, what if collections exceed payments?"

"Excellent question! If collections exceed payments, they owe the government that money and—if payments exceed collections—the government owes you. Technically, the timing is when you invoice people, and when people invoice you." Dan sat back, a grin on his mug. Paul looked confused, but only mildly so. "Anyway," he continued, "the restaurant could have a full year to pay the net GST they collected."

"What about employees?"

"A similar thing happens—the business withholds tax, CPP and EI from the employee's cheques—then they get a couple of weeks to send in payroll remittances. So—again—a cash business like a restaurant has a huge short-term cash advantage. But—if they aren't profitable—the money isn't sitting in the bank when it's time to pay the government."

"Wouldn't someone get in a lot of trouble for not paying?"

Dan nodded. "You're right about that—the rules are tough. The government can collect from individuals even if they were only a director of the company. However, in the short run, when a restaurant is in deep trouble, many owners lean on the only big creditor they know—the government. It's a shame, and the result is a lot of people go bankrupt.

The point is you need to be profitable but, depending on the industry and how much you grow, you also have to survive the cash flow challenge." He glanced at the coffeemaker. "If you have time, I'll put on a pot of coffee, and I'll walk you through it . . ."

Paul agreed, then called Mandy to let her know he would be home within the hour. "She told me to learn as much as I can!"

"Smart woman!"

Five minutes later, Dan sneaked two cups of coffee before it was done brewing, handing one to Paul. "So, what don't you understand?"

Paul accepted the mug, subconsciously checking it to make sure it had enough cream. "I think I get the basic concept, but how do I calculate the size of the problem I might have?"

"You look at everything you have to pay in the first month as well as what might come in—then do the same thing for the second month. Then, the third. Of course, you can't just have a negative balance in the bank—you have to cover that shortfall somehow. You'll need to cover each new shortfall until you get to a month where the receipts exceed the payments." Dan waited to see if Paul had any questions. "Remember a couple of other things—you have your own personal bills to pay, so don't forget the need to draw out a bit of money. Also remember if the business manages to borrow, don't forget the repayments on the debt—including interest." Dan wasn't sure, but he thought he saw Paul's left eye start to glaze.

He was right. "It seems to me, growing the business at a slower rate may be the best way to go. I can see how all of this can get out of control . . ."

"Indeed. If you grow quickly, doing a monthly projection may not be enough. Some companies do a weekly or daily projection—yes, it's a massive amount of work, but your survival might depend on it." He watched Paul nod his understanding. "Finally," he offered, "watch out for critical assumptions. The most common problem is you may have assumed you will collect in 60 days, and it turns out to be 90 or 120 days—the inability to collect a big receivable on time kills far too many construction companies . . ."

Paul thought about the plumbing companies he knew were in the top tier of success. "Okay—so if I were starting a plumbing company, what are my options?" He hesitated. "My *best* options . . ."

"Well—you mentioned one, and that was sticking to small jobs, thereby growing the business slowly. Your second choice? Borrow from a bank—but they will want great security, usually in the form of equity in your home. Forget about offering RRSP investments as security—the bank can't use them. So, that leaves the third option—borrowing from the 'three Fs'—family, fools, and friends."

Paul shook his head vehemently. "No way am I ever doing that—I have to tell you, this is sobering stuff." He paused. "Let me see if I understand you—overall, you're saying even if I am profitable, I could fail because of a cash flow crisis. "

Dan nodded.

"And, if I borrow on my house or from my family and the big receivable doesn't come through when projected, I could face losing my house as well as damaging family relationships . . ."

Dan felt for Paul—his years as a financial consultant told him Paul was, perhaps, second thinking his plan of opening his own plumbing business. "It's a lot to think about, isn't it? You can see how not everyone is cut out to take these kinds of tremendous risks . . ."

"Truthfully, I don't like the idea of having to turn down great jobs because I might not have the cash to pay the up-front costs. That—would be frustrating . . ."

Shortly before they called it a night, Dan encouraged Paul to talk to Nick, his boss. Chances were good he would have war stories from his early days, and they would certainly offer Paul the chance to learn.

As the two men stood at the back door, Paul turned to Dan with a more serious-than-usual look. "You know—I guess I didn't really understand how tough opening my own business will be. It kind of seems like I was making a decision before I knew what I have to do—all I basically knew was I have to find work." Paul looked at his shoes, slightly shaking his head. "But—obviously—that's just the starting point.

Chapter Seven—Cash Flow vs. Profit

You warned me about preparing a business plan, and you said it was a serious exercise." He glanced back at Dan as crisp night air slapped his face. "I guess that means if I can't prove to myself how this will work, I just shouldn't go into business—is that it?"

Dan knew he was dishing up a bitter pill, but he knew without question Paul would make the right decision for him and his family.

"Right," he answered, following Paul down the walk. "However, by doing your homework you might avoid bankruptcy, losing your house, and destroying key relationships. The rewards can be high—but the risks aren't minor." He paused as they reached the front gate. "By the way, if you read or hear people talking about new businesses having 'insufficient equity' or being 'undercapitalized,'—well, this is what they're referring to . . ."

Paul turned toward his house. "I get it . . ."

"One last thing—does Nick ever talk about the bonding company?

Paul nodded. "He has—I know it has something to do with his being able to bid on certain jobs because he is well-established. I gather it's about his reputation . . ."

"In a way—reputation is important, but so is having the cash behind you."

Paul stopped and turned, blowing on his hands for warmth.

Dan noticed. "I'll make this snappy—when a customer insists you have bonding, it means if you bid too low or—for some reason—you can't finish the job, the customer can turn to the bonding company to get the job done. Of course, the bonding company can't be paying claims very often, or they will be out of business. So, as you might expect, before the bonding company backs you, they will want to see a lot of your own cash in the business."

Paul glanced over his shoulder toward his house. "I have to go—but, it sounds as if I have a lot of homework to do before I decide on opening my own business." He extended his hand. "Thanks again—you have no idea how much I appreciate it!"

Dan returned the handshake. "Any time, my friend—any time, at all!" He watched Paul turn up the walk to his house. "And, thanks for the water heater!"

Chapter Eight

A Business Consultant's Best Advice

"I think it's a good idea! Harry and a puppy will bond..." Mandy bounced their son on her knee, as she presented her case for a new family member.

"Seriously? A dog?" Paul looked at her in disbelief. "How on earth are you going to take care of a new dog? You have enough to do, and I'm going to be putting in extra hours so we can save money..."

"I know—but, will you just trust me on this one?"

In that moment, Paul knew his well-thought out argument was in vain. Mandy had her heart set on a new puppy, and there was no talking her out of it.

He sighed. "What kind of puppy?"

A huge smile sprang to life as she realized what her husband was saying. "I know of a little French Bulldog puppy

—people down the street have them . . ."

"Cost? I don't feel like paying for a dog . . ."

"That's the best part—it's free!"

There went his last defense—down in flames. He looked at his wife and son, realizing there was nothing he could do. "Alright," he grinned. "What are you going to name it?"

"I have no idea—I think we should name it according to personality . . . what do you think?"

"This, my sweet wife, is your gig . . ." He stood, kissing her and his son on their heads. "I have to do that side job—I'll be back in a couple of hours . . ."

****

Franklin arrived in rather ceremonious fashion, instantly proving Paul's concerns. Turned out the little puppy had a few more years on him—undisciplined years, at that. Paul pegged him at two or three at the least and, clearly, his previous owners spent little time with training. And, as Paul took Franklin for a walk during his first week with them, he questioned Mandy's sanity.

He was lost in thought when Dan met him at his sidewalk gate. "What's with the dog," he asked, grinning.

Chapter Eight—A Business Consultant's Best Advice

"Mandy's idea—she and Harry are in love with him . . ."

"What's his name?"

"Franklin . . ."

Dan looked at Paul, expressionless. "Franklin?"

"Yep—Franklin . . ."

Dan wisely assessed the time wasn't right to discuss the benefits of having an unruly French Bulldog—a change of subject was in order.

"So—what else is new?"

Paul tugged on the leash, praying the dog would sit down. "New? Nothing really—but do you remember the other day when I told you the most valuable advice a plumber can give is to turn off your main water supply when you go on holidays?"

"Indeed, I do—it's downright good advice. As you know, I had flood damage a couple of times, and it is almost as bad as a fire . . ."

Paul nodded. "So—I was thinking . . . we talked about cash flow vs. profit, but I'm guessing you have a million more tips. What else do I need to know?"

Dan thought for a minute. "Okay—here's one. Don't undercharge. I didn't bring it up to you because it seems to be less of a problem for the trades . . ."

Paul heard something behind him, turning to see Mandy and Harry coming toward them.

"What on earth are you doing standing out here in the cold?" She shifted Harry on her hip, adjusting his teeny hat.

"Are you coming to rescue Franklin," Paul teased, holding out the leash. "Why don't you take him back inside with you—I need to talk to Dan for a sec . . ."

"You're just trying to get out of walking the dog!" She laughed, but she knew her statement had a ring of truth.

"Maybe . . ." He held out the leash as his wife again shifted Harry, silently thinking her son was going to be a big boy—he was heavy!

Dan gave Paul the thumbs up as Mandy grabbed the leash, heading for the house. "Nicely done . . ."

Paul watched his wife head up the steps, making sure she made it inside okay. "Okay—where were we?"

"I was about to give you an example of another piece of financial wisdom . . ." He laughed, motioning for Paul to following him inside.

Once settled in his den, he took a long look at Paul, thinking how impressed he was by Paul's determination to plot out a successful life for his family. It was unusual—*most young people don't consider retirement until it's too late*, he thought as he grabbed two beers from the mini fridge.

He sat, making himself comfortable in his favorite chair. "Well, I did about 600 personal tax returns a year for people who had no company, and that was all I did for them. I don't mind telling you my partner gave me a bit of a bad time about it—he knew I enjoyed the work, but he was convinced I wasn't charging enough. So, he suggested I pop off an email to let them know I would be charging them 25% more unless the tax work needed dropped significantly."

"How many complained, or left?"

Dan thought for a moment, recalling the response to

his new fees. "As I recall, no one complained—at least they weren't serious complaints—and I don't believe I lost any of them. But, of course, the reason was I was definitely under charging, and they knew it." He paused for a swig, savoring his favorite honey ale. "But, do the math—previously, I charged $200 per return and, after the fee hike, I charged $240."

Paul's mind raced with quick calculations. "On 600 returns at $40 each extra profit? Holy cow! That's $24,000 per year!"

Dan laughed. "Indeed! Now think about this—my career spanned forty years—that's roughly a million bucks that could have gone to my retirement savings!"

Paul's expression betrayed his thoughts. "You literally gave money away . . ."

"I did—yes, I corrected the situation in the middle of my career, but it was silly way to throw half a mil out the window!"

"Did your business grow less?"

"Maybe—but I was already working all I could. Tax season is largely only a month long, and I can only work so many hours.

"So—you wasted money because you didn't realize you weren't charging enough. How will I know if I'm charging what I should? Once I have my own business, I mean . . ."

"This part is interesting—in my consulting work, I asked business clients to identify their biggest problem."

Paul's eyebrows furrowed a little as he struggled to understand. "So, if they said they were working too hard . . ."

Dan finished his thought for him. "... I suspected they were undercharging."

Paul still looked a little confused. "Is that always true?"

"No—some things are extremely price sensitive..."

Paul nodded. "Right—like a liter of gas is the same price all over..."

"Unfortunately, price sensitivity and technology are driving many small Canadian businesses out of business..."

"You mean the mom and pop'ers?"

"Exactly—take book stores. I had a client about ten years ago who owned a very cool little book store in a neat shopping area—lots of traffic but not enough sales. He was selling at the suggested retail price, and he knew a lot about books and people loved his book suggestions."

"That doesn't sound bad to me—he should have been fine. What happened?"

"It was simple—people got to know they could get books cheaper at the big stores like Wal-Mart or Costco..."

"So—people took ideas from your client, and bought their book elsewhere?"

"Many did, but not all—however, his problem included getting killed on the buying side. His wholesalers were often charging him more than people could buy the books for at Costco. In fact, at times, he bought at Costco."

Paul placed his beer on the end table. "Did the Internet and electronic books cause him trouble?"

Dan shook his head. "No—but only because he went out of business before the Internet was relevant..."

Chapter Eight—A Business Consultant's Best Advice

Paul looked slightly bummed. "Just thinking about it, that must apply to many things we buy—wherever we buy something, few small businesses survive." He thought for a moment before continuing. "Record stores, for example—movie rentals, mom and pop grocery stores. Gas stations. Even sporting goods!"

"That's right—people love having these little businesses around but, without regular support, the few we have left will disappear."

"It seems like small towns are doing better keeping their local businesses . . ."

"Sometimes—but it really depends on the town. It's like the town is best to stay the same size. If the town grows big enough for box stores to come in, the local businesses die. And, of course, if the town is shrinking, it's just a matter of time—it's too small to support those retailers."

"Good thing I'm not going into retail—I'll have enough to worry about just getting a plumbing business up and running." He thought for a moment. "In the mall, it seems there's a lot of variety—such as ladies clothing stores. There are a bunch of them . . ."

Dan stood. "Another beer?"

Paul considered not having one, but then he remembered Franklin. "Yep—one for the road, please . . ."

Dan grabbed two more brews from the fridge, handing one to his guest after twisting off the top. "Will it surprise you to know how many of them are owned by giant companies?"

Paul arched his eyebrows.

"Outside of small towns," Dan continued, "retail is dominated by big business . . ."

"Are you saying no one should start a retail business?"

Dan again shook his head. "No—I wouldn't go that far. But, I would be very careful—anyone starting a business needs to find areas where service is an important component. For example, if I were selling computers or crafts, I would be putting on training classes . . ."

"I understand your point about undercharging—but, to be blunt, I'm not interested in retail . . ."

Dan took a sip. "I understand. But, think about this—when my water heater broke, I had little interest in whether it cost $800 or $1,200. What I cared about was how fast I could get it fixed—and, I wanted the job done well. Trust is an issue . . ."

"But, if you found out you paid too much, you probably wouldn't go back to that plumber . . ."

"True—but I think there's a difference between recognizing something was a bit expensive, and feeling ripped off . . ."

Paul thought about Dan's comment before answering. "You're probably right—I think most people know the person they hire is trying to make a living. Especially when they know them personally . . ."

Dan nodded. "The definition of a business I like best is *selling products, or providing services at a price that results in a profit.* In other words, selling steak sandwiches at $6 isn't a business—but, if you're selling them for $20, they better be amazing! So, anything under $12 probably means you're selling them too cheap." He paused, thinking he heard Linda come in from her weekly meeting.

"Lin?" He listened. Nothing. He chuckled, glancing at Paul. "False alarm . . ."

"I thought I heard her, too. Which reminds me—I better be heading home." He checked his watch. "How about ten more minutes?"

"Perfect—I only have a few more things for advice. So—speaking of profit, I had a restaurant client many years ago who didn't understand the need for profit. His portion sizes were crazy, and diners took home more food than they ate. Not only that, few ordered appetizers or desserts because they knew the main courses were monsters. And, his prices were low even though the portions were large. You can imagine he had customers lining up at the door to get in—even at midweek."

"What happened?"

"Well, as you might guess, he eventually went out of business. I think his ego needed to see that huge line streaming out his door every day for some reason. It's too bad, too—in effect, it was sort of a reverse rip-off when the customers were ripping off the owner."

"To me, it seems like he was stealing customers from other restaurants . . ."

"Or, grocery stores—it was almost that bad."

Paul thought about Dan's story before finally commenting. "But that had to do with ego—what about other people. Why do they make the mistake of charging too little?"

Dan took his final swig for the evening. "I think—sometimes—for established businesses, it has to do with fear. The fear of someone else taking customers . . ."

"What do you mean?"

"Well let's say you sell ping pong balls for $1, and you sell

1 million a year. Then, let's say they cost 80 cents, and your overhead is roughly fixed at $80,000 . . ."

"So your profit is $120,000 . . ."

"Very good—now, let's say someone else has a sale. So you figure—out of fear that you should cut your price by 10%—the extra volume will ensure you make the same, or more money."

Paul questioned Dan's thinking. "Isn't that pretty unlikely? Wouldn't you have to sell twice as much? Unless your customers were extremely price sensitive, it wouldn't work . . ."

Dan thought for a moment. "There probably are elements of overhead that would rise a bit, so maybe you have to increase your volume by more than 2 times." He paused. "Anyway, the point is—sometimes you need to weather a storm. Just don't undercharge . . ."

"Are you telling me you can influence customers to be less price sensitive? How does that work?"

"The first thing is you need to fill a particular need brilliantly well. When your customers love what you're doing, they're unlikely to complain too much about price.

Second, once in a while, do a little something for free—people love it. High-end restaurants understand this concept well, and they'll often hand out something like a small free drink at the end of the meal. It helps ease the shock when the bill comes . . .

Another example—my tire shop changes winter and summer tires for free—of course, I always buy my tires there and, I admit, I probably get a bit casual regarding prices.

Last, promote loyalty anyway you can. I know it's

Chapter Eight—A Business Consultant's Best Advice

expensive, but a few times a week I buy a latte. My local guy charges the same as the International chain—but, the local guy makes me a free latte if I fill my gift card for $30 or more. So, I'm loyal to him, for the most part . . ."

"Is this relevant to commercial construction? We have to bid all the time . . ."

"Very much so—obviously, you need to win bids, but you don't want to win everything you're bidding on."

Paul hesitated, thinking about Dan's example. "Because that means we're bidding too low . . ."

"Bingo! That's right! If you're winning all of your bids, up your prices to the point you lose the bid once in awhile."

"Well, I know that's true—sometimes we get the bid even though we aren't the lowest price."

Dan stood. "So—that's the value of a great reputation. Odds are the general contractor tried those bottom feeders before, and it wasn't worth it."

Paul rose, and headed for the door. "As always, I learned something—I like having a personal consultant!"

Dan laughed, watching Paul head down the sidewalk. "And give Franklin a pat for me . . ."

He couldn't quite see what Dan gestured.

Chapter Nine

Family, and Other Stuff

No one could believe Harry turned one—it seemed as if only a couple of months passed since they brought him home from the hospital. With an almost toddler in the house, Dan and Linda figured their neighbors had their hands full—but the time finally came when Dan decided he needed to have a conversation with Paul about the financial logistics of raising a family. There was no doubt he could use it—especially when he and Linda suspected Mandy was pregnant again.

Unfortunately, his conversation had to wait a week due to Harry's catching a nasty cold. Paul and Mandy were sharing late night nursing duties, and Dan could well imagine Paul didn't have the time nor inclination to talk about money.

He was right.

It was a good ten days before he had the opportunity to snag Paul as he took the infamous Franklin for a stroll.

"Hey, neighbor! It's been a while!" He took the leash while Paul flipped through the mail. "How's Harry? Linda told me he was sick . . ."

Paul nodded, taking back possession of the incorrigible bulldog. "He's getting better, but he gave us a scare—all we could do was hold him, and get him through it . . ." Paul held up his hand, clutching the mail. "Nothing but bills . . ."

"I know," Dan agreed. "Having kids is tough on family finances—I imagine you noticed your income dropped when Mandy stayed home to take care of Harry. I recall she wanted to start her own business—how's that working out?"

"It's not—she hasn't had time to turn around."

"That's the way it was when we were starting our family—Linda wound up quitting her job."

"Did you have maternity benefits?"

"Sure—even so, the family income toppled. Expenses go up—not too much at first, but they'll rise quickly after a while."

"How so?"

"Well—either Mandy stays away from work for a long time, or you pay child care." Dan noticed the look on Paul's face when he mentioned child care. "Even if she wants to have a home business, it's not as easy as it seems . . ."

Paul nodded as Franklin started barking at another dog. He looked at Dan, rolling his eyes. "We found that out . . ."

"And, that's not all of it—if you decide to have more kids, you may need a bigger house. Before we had kids, our house was under 800 square feet—and, while we could have raised kids in a small house, we moved. People often buy bigger, newer vehicles, as well."

"I get it about the cars—two or three kids? The minivan or SUV sounds like a good idea . . ."

"Then you have insurance—that's another issue. The second you have kids, life and disability insurance come into the picture." It wasn't Dan's style to pry, but he wanted to make sure Paul and Mandy considered life and disability insurance—both could be a lifesaver down the road.

"I have insurance from work . . ."

"Good—then there's one more personal issue. You talk about starting your own business and odds are—in the early days—you will work pretty crazy hours, and be under a lot of stress."

"I know—I thought about that. Mandy will be at home with Harry, wondering why I'm working sixty hours a week. But, we talked about it, and she knows she'll need to sacrifice time with me . . ."

"Then she'll be the most understanding wife in the world—trust me, feeling as if she's raising the kids by herself will wear thin. And, if you have more children, you can take that frustration and—well, you can double it. Or, triple it!"

Paul tugged on Franklin's leash to remind him he wasn't free to roam the streets. "Right—certainly issues worth thinking about . . ." He looked at Dan, then at his house. The front porch light flickered on, and time to talk was limited. He turned back to his friend. "I'd like your opinion on this, if you have time . . ."

Dan nodded he did.

"A buddy of mine," Paul continued, "is in real trouble. He started a business, and it isn't going to work—frankly, I think he's considering bankruptcy."

I really hate to hear that, Dan thought before answering. "Well, he should talk to a trustee—he may be able to negotiate, especially if he doesn't have too many creditors."

"As I understand it, his only significant problem is the lease he signed. His business is sports trivia—he sells people's stuff on consignment, so he can just give the goods back to their owners. On some stuff, he's having a blow-out sale, but the kicker is he signed a five-year year lease. His monthly base rent is $3,000, and operating costs are $2,000—but, with four years to go, he owes almost $250,000."

Dan winced. "That's a good chunk of change . . ."

"No kidding! Maybe he can sublet to someone else—but, he told me he may have to do so at, perhaps, a lower rent, pay commissions, and he might not get anyone in there for a year or two . . ."

"Unfortunately, your friend's story is a common one—and, it's sad. Did he incorporate a company?"

"Yes—he knew he could limit liability by incorporating, and that's why he was willing to take the risk . . ."

"Ah—let me guess— personal guarantees."

"Yep—the landlord would only deal with him if signed a personal guarantee. So, if the company can't make the payments, the landlord can go after him personally . . ."

Dan shook his head, thinking about how many times he hears stories similar to Paul's friend's. "It seems people can't imagine their business isn't going to succeed, so they don't think through what will happen if the business fails."

He paused. "He should also see a lawyer on the off chance the guarantee isn't valid . . ."

Franklin was clearly ready to experience the comforts of home, so Paul figured they should call it a day. "Thanks—I'll let him know what you suggest—he knows I talk to you about these things, and I think he'll be glad to hear what you think . . ."

"Ah! My reputation precedes me!"

****

Harry's birthday came and went, and Paul and Mandy couldn't believe he was an official toddler. Of course, he occupied most of Mandy's days and, as Dan thought might happen, Paul was spending more time doing side jobs in preparation for opening his own business. He figured he needed to bring in as much money as possible, but he started to think about something he never considered previously—a partner.

When the word 'partner' cropped up, Mandy wasn't too thrilled about it. She heard stories of partners breaking up families, marriages, and businesses, and she was pretty sure she didn't want any part of it.

"But, maybe we should just think about it," Paul suggested as they enjoyed a cup of hot chocolate at the kitchen table. "Dan told me a partnership is like a financial marriage, so we'd have to go into it with our eyes wide open."

"I just don't understand why we need to consider bringing someone else into your business..." No, it was safe to say Mandy didn't like the idea, at all.

"You know how many times I talked to Dan about starting our own business, but, I gotta tell you—it's stories like his that make me second guess our decision."

"You talked to him about the possibility of a partner?"

"Yes—and, no matter how much I don't want to hear it, I trust him. He knows what he's talking about . . ."

"What did he say?"

"He said a partnership is like a marriage, but it has a much higher divorce rate. And, he should know—he had partners during his career, and it was terrific most of the time. But, not always—plus, he said getting out of one of those failed partnerships can be tough."

"Tough how?"

"Well, sometimes the business is fine, but the relationship just doesn't work."

"But, why wouldn't it work? If you bring someone into a business, it seems to me you should have a good idea of what they're like . . ."

Paul sensed Mandy's getting upset. "I know—I agree. But Dan said there might be different strengths or styles. And, while those differences can be great, we often fail to appreciate someone who operates differently than we do."

"I guess it makes sense—but, I don't know . . ."

Chapter Nine—Family and Other Stuff

"Okay—here's an example. Imagine I start a plumbing company with someone named Joe. Both of us bring different things to the table—I bring marketing with general contractors, as well as recruiting new plumbers to join our company." He paused, waiting for a response from Mandy. Nothing. " But, Joe," he continued, "is the guy who is great at supervising the jobs."

"So? That doesn't sound so bad . . ."

"Agreed—but, according to Dan, both of us may feel our own role is more important. Maybe—during times of stress—you say things to each other you shouldn't. One thing leads to another, and we're not talking . . ."

Mandy thought about the scenario. "So I'm right—we don't need to consider a partner . . ."

"Maybe—but I'm still not convinced."

"Well, let's just say you do decide on a partner—how do you avoid the business divorce?"

"Dan said partners who aren't getting along can try counseling. Communicating better. Appreciating each other. But, he also said those techniques don't work very often."

Mandy shook her head. "Then what?"

"Shareholder agreements—Dan says they're standard when doing business with someone."

"I've heard of them . . ."

"Me, too. Dan explained a shareholder's agreement is something partners sign early on—before the business starts, or at least in the honeymoon stage. There's one key item . . ."

"And, that is?"

"The shotgun clause..."

Mandy winced. "That sounds pretty harsh..."

"I know, right? This is how Dan explained it to me—let's say after two years, Joe and I have to go our separate ways. I could offer to buy Joe out—however, my offer isn't high enough."

"Can't you force him to sell?"

Paul laughed. "That's what I thought! But, the answer is no—we can't. But, the way a shotgun works is if he says no, he must buy me out for the same price..."

"Mandy smiled at her husband. "Okay—I'm totally confused..."

"I was, too, until I understood I would need to pick the buyout number carefully, since I wouldn't know if I were buying or selling. Dan says that's the beauty of it—and it works pretty well if there are two people who own the company 50-50—they'll have about the same economic situation."

Suddenly, Mandy cocked her ear toward the baby's room. "Did you just hear Harry," she asked, a concerned look on her face."

Paul listened carefully. "I don't think so..."

She listened intently, finally thinking it was something outside.

Or, Franklin.

"Why is economic situation important," she asked, her mind again on their conversation.

"I asked that same question—say you have a clear title

house, and $500,000 in the bank, but Joe has very little. Maybe a fair number for the total value of the business is one million..."

"Okay..."

"So, I could offer him say $300,000 because I can afford to buy him out, but he can't afford to match my offer."

"What if you have multiple owners?"

"I guess that's a possibility—as I understand it, if there are five owners, the possibility exists the others may think I should go. None of them wants me as a partner—fair or unfair.

"What?"

"Hear me out—so, if they offer me $150,000, I can accept that, or buy them all out for $600,000 . . . that's the shotgun clause . . ."

"Well, I'm going to stick to my original thought—I don't think you need to consider a partner—or, partners," Mandy said, emphasizing the 's' on 'partners.'

"I'm not saying I'm going to seek a partner—anyway, as Dan explains it, shotgun clauses aren't perfect, but they do get something done. Sometimes, he said, just knowing the shotgun clause is available motivates people to get on with a fair negotiation. He says, overall, shareholders agreements are a big topic—and he cautioned me that if we're thinking about going into business with someone, we need to discuss all the possibilities. We can't simply discuss how great it will be, and we need to be aware the business can fail."

"I think it sounds like a dreadful idea—but, you're the one who knows more about it than I, and I trust you to make the right decision—after talking it over with me, of course!"

Paul grinned at his wife. "I know I sounded pretty negative, and I'm sorry about that. I do think having our own business can be terrific—we just need to be informed, and we can't live in a dream world. New businesses are high reward, but high risk goes along with it." Paul paused, trying to remember something he saw long ago. "I can't remember when it was, but I saw a cartoon that really made an impact on me..."

"A cartoon?"

"Yeah—two guys were robbing a bank, and about twenty police officers charged in from every window and door. The one robber yells to the other, 'Switch to plan B!'"

After a moment of thinking about it, Mandy wasn't quite sure of the point of his story. "I don't get it..."

"The joke is there is no realistic plan B! Having a good plan B can pay huge dividends—but, if plan B sounds terrible, you may want to rethink things."

Paul was right—many times, you can't see a good outcome from failure, but surely that's motivation to go over your business plan again to ensure it's airtight!

Chapter Ten

Incorporating a Company

Mandy's pregnancy scare was exactly that—a scare. Although she and Paul were slightly disappointed, both realized they needed to get a little more time under their belts with one kid before increasing the size of their family.

Card night with Dan and Linda took a back seat as both couples dug their heels in to get through the winter. Colder than usual, Paul had his share of busted pipes and water heaters, and he found his usual weekend morphed from something doable to something causing stress. He felt as if he were missing Harry's important steps in growing up, and the need to open his own company rose to the forefront.

For the first time in months, Paul and Mandy got a babysitter, meeting Dan and Linda at a restaurant with the best food in town.

"I can't believe I'm not home making dinner!" Mandy

laughed as she squeezed fresh lemon into her water. "And, I can tell you right now I'm not having chicken!"

"What's wrong with chicken?" Linda looked at her friend, a quizzical look on her face.

"Oh, there's nothing wrong with it—I'm tired of it! I swear we have chicken five times a week!"

Paul laughed, and nodded. "It's cheap!" He glanced at his wife. "Mandy can get more out of one scrawny chicken than you can imagine!"

Dan glanced at his wife, recalling the days when they were young. "That's good—frugality will pay off!" After a quick sip of his drink, he sat back, looking at his young neighbors. "So—are you still thinking about opening your own business?"

Paul nodded. "Yep—I'm learning as much as I can about incorporating. Unfortunately, that requires free time . . ." He clasped Mandy's hand. "And, the free time I have, I want to spend with my family . . ."

"I don't blame you—the days of enjoying Harry as he grows will be gone soon enough . . ." He paused, thinking of his own grown children. Paul thought he recognized a sadness in his friend's eyes as he put his arm around Linda's shoulder.

"I know—so, I'm thinking about incorporating more than ever . . ."

Mandy and Linda glanced at each other. "Shall we?"

"Yep—I'm with you. I'll call the babysitter, too . . ."

Within moments they disappeared into the depths of the restaurant, leaving their men to discuss business.

Chapter Ten—Incorporating a Company

Dan laughed. "Well—that was subtle!" He raised his glass in a toast. "To . . . talking business!"

Paul grinned, making himself comfortable in the oversized dining chair. "So, Professor—what do I need to know?"

"About incorporating?"

"Yep—the first thing I need to know is do I need to incorporate immediately? When I open the doors to the business, I mean . . ."

"Well, normally, I caution people about incorporating immediately because it costs more money to file tax returns. And, the other problem is losses get trapped inside the company—you can't flow the losses out to your personal tax returns. But, in your case, I imagine you will be totally committed to the company—if you keep the company small and don't take a salary, I imagine you won't lose money. If you do, it can be a real mess since Mandy's wages are minimal."

Paul fiddled with the cocktail straw in his drink. "Interesting—when we talked a few months ago, we discussed limited liability. I have to admit, I like the sound of it . . ."

"Why? What appeals to you about limited liability?"

"I'm not sure—that's why I need to learn about incorporating. The thing that scares me witless is being sued if I agree to a personal guarantee . . ."

Dan nodded. "You're probably wise to be leery—and, don't forget creditors can go after everything the company owns . . ." He hesitated as he thought of Paul's possible pitfalls. "So, realistically, failing can be a real mess—but, if you avoid guarantees, at least your personal credit should survive . . ."

"You sound as if surviving isn't a given . . ."

Dan sighed. "It never is . . ."

Paul spied the girls close to the front entrance, engrossed in conversation with someone who must have been a long lost friend. He watched as his wife broke into a huge grin, then place the palm of her hand on the person's tummy. "From the looks of it, the girls found an acquaintance on their way back to the table," he informed Dan.

"Good—I don't want to be talking business while the girls are with us—I'm pretty sure they wouldn't consider it a good night out . . ."

"Agreed—I think they'll be another few minutes, however—so if I did incorporate right away, should Mandy and I own it 50-50?"

"Not really—a better structure is to have a least two classes of shares. You might own Class A common shares, and she might own Class B common shares—that way, you can pay dividends in any combination that suits you."

"Really?" Paul picked up the menu, then put it down immediately. "So if I were working at it a lot harder than Mandy, she could be paid as much as me or even more?"

"Technically, yes—but, to clarify, it only applies to dividends, not salaries. By being incorporated, the company will make the money and pay corporate income tax. The Federal rate is 10.5% and the Alberta rate is only 3% . . ."

Paul noticed his friend needed a refill, so both opted to go with something without alcohol. "How about two iced teas," he asked the waiter as the girls took their seats at the table. The server smiled, promising to be right back.

Mandy had a grin the size of Alberta plastered on her

face, obviously bursting with some sort of great news. "You'll never guess who I saw as we were heading back to the table!" she exclaimed as she gave her husband a peck on the cheek.

Dan laughed as he stood to pull out his wife's chair. "I give—who?"

"Christine Johnson! And, you'll never believe this—she's pregnant!" She didn't wait for her husband's response. "You'd never recognize her—even though we're the same age, she looks so . . . much older."

"Maybe that's because you haven't changed a bit!" He laughed, knowing his wife would get the joke.

"Good answer—but, really, she looks as if she's been put through the wringer . . ."

Paul thought for a second. "Didn't her husband have something to with an electric company?"

"Yep—Christine told me it didn't make it, though . . ."

Paul sat back, stunned at his wife's news. If he remembered correctly, her husband was a smart guy—it didn't make sense. Paul couldn't help feeling a sting—if that guy couldn't make it, what makes him think he will?

****

Paul and Dan didn't have an opportunity to resume their conversation until snowbanks were beginning to melt. Somehow, Paul made it through the busy season relatively unscathed, and he and Mandy finally decided it was time for him to move forward with owning their own business. With the stress of making the decision put to rest, Paul knew he had to spend as much time as possible with Dan. He gave himself six months and—when he really thought about it—it really wasn't a lot of time.

Dan graciously offered to get together with him a couple of times a week when possible, teaching him the basics of becoming his own businessman. It was an exciting time, but Paul and Mandy would be lying if they said they weren't a little fearful of the whole darned thing.

Parked in Dan's kitchen, coffee in hand, Dan picked up where they left off the evening they met for dinner several weeks previously. "Actually, as corporation tax rates go, all the western provinces are terrific . . ." He glanced at Paul to verify his friend remembered their earlier conversation. "If you recall, at the restaurant we were talking about Federal taxes being 10.5%, and Alberta is 3%—that's a considerable difference . . ."

"I do remember—I'm glad I live in Alberta! But . . ." he scrunched his forehead as if he were working through a problem. "But, then . . . we pay a bunch of personal tax when we get the dividend—right?"

Dan nodded. "However, you might be surprised by how little it might be," he commented. "But, let's keep going . . ."

Paul took a sip of coffee, then poured in a dab of cream. "That sounds simple enough—what else do I have to worry about?

"Well, make sure you and Mandy actually pay for your

Chapter Ten—Incorporating a Company

shares—and, be certain both of you have your own money to pay for them. Both of you are employed, so that shouldn't be much of a problem—the cost of the shares will be nominal." He paused for a moment. "Maybe a hundred bucks, each. Of course, it goes without saying you need to keep all documents pertaining to incorporation—you never know when you're going to need to show them to a tax auditor . . ." He stood, motioning for his friend to follow. "Step into my office . . ."

Minutes later, both were sitting in front of Dan's computer monitor. "This modeling software is incredible—it will help clarify how everything works."

"Cool! Let's get to it!" Dan nodded, clicking the mouse button twice.

"So," Paul began, "lets assume my company is making $200,000. That's realistic—and, let's also assume Mandy and I don't have additional income . . ."

"Okay—now I need to know what you have to take from the company for living expenses . . ."

Paul thought for a moment before answering. "Well—about $6,000 a month sounds like enough—we'll need to build the company up as soon as we can, and I'm not forgetting what you taught me about cash flow—the cash will come in slower than the payments." He paused to consider possible scenarios. "Also, I'd like to grow by taking on bigger jobs—that means employing more plumbers. The more the company grows, the more I'll need the profits to finance growth—right? As I see it, such a plan is critically important for two to five years.

Dan nodded, and clicked again. "Got it—let me put in a salary option and a dividend option to see how they compare. In both cases, I'll make sure you have $6,000 a month to live on . . ." He turned to Paul. "This will take about five minutes,

I think—maybe less..."

He was right on the money. Five minutes later, the screen showed them everything they needed to know. Dan scooted forward so he could tilt the screen a bit more toward Paul. "Check this out—from the model, I doubt you would go the salary route unless you were going to buy RRSPs..."

"We talked about those, too, quite a while back..."

"I remember—look here..." He pointed to the screen. "While I used salaries of 50-50, I'd be concerned about justifying your salary unless Mandy works in the company full time in a valuable role." He glanced at Paul. "But, for now, we'll just use a salary of $60,000 each—that will entitle you to buy RRSPs of $21,600. That's 18% of $120,000... so, with those big RRSP deductions, the total company and personal taxes are about $3,700 less than if you were paid you dividends."

"But you said you don't like the salary route—why not?"

"Well let's look at where the money goes in both cases—using salaries, you guys get $6,000 a month, or $72,000 per year for personal spending. Total taxes are $26,200—so we have almost $101,800 left ($200,000 profit less $72,000 for spending as well as less income taxes of $26,200. That leaves $101,800..." Again he glanced at Paul—so far, so good. "So—that's the total that will go into one of three places. CPP gets $10,200, and RRSPs get $21,600—only $70,000 is left in the company.

Paul considered Dan's example—to him, it wasn't the easiest thing to figure out. "That doesn't sound too bad, but I'd rather have more profits retained in the company for growth." He paused, thinking about the situation. "From what you said previously—months ago—the cash going to CPP and RRSPs is unavailable to the company even as security. Does that mean dividends work out a bit better?"

Dan grinned. "A lot better! The personal spending is still $72,000, and the taxes are a bit higher at $29,900—so, out of the profit of $200,000, that leaves $98,100. But, since nothing goes to CPP or RRSPs, the whole $98,100 stays inside the company. That's about 40% more than the $70,500 you get when using salaries . . ."

Paul tossed it around for several minutes, but there was something not right. "Something seems wrong here—didn't you say the company tax rate is 13.5%?"

"Right—so the company income tax is $27,000 . . ."

"But when using dividends, you said the total tax is only $29,900. Does that mean the personal taxes for both of us is only $2,900?"

"Indeed—amazing isn't it?"

Paul was still doubtful. "As usual, I guess we'll pay more one day . . ."

Dan nodded. "That's right—you will. But, if tax rates don't change and you continue to live on $6,000 per month, you will continue to pay the low taxes even in retirement. That's a big advantage over folks where their retirement depends on CPP and RRSPs—their taxes will be a lot higher. A nice little hidden benefit, don't you think?" He thought before breaking into a grin. "You might say you need to save less to retire on since your future taxes are less . . ."

The pessimist in Paul made an appearance as he wondered how everything would work for Mandy and him. And, as usual, he expected the worst. "Sounds great, but what's the downside?"

Dan took a swig of coffee. "There's always a downside,

isn't there?" Another sip. "The truth is accountants can be reluctant to recommend the dividend route to many of their clients.

"I don't get it—why?"

"Because once the company doesn't need the money for growth, you can end up with a lot of cash sitting in the company's chequing account—a tempting situation. But, remember—don't fall into the pit of blowing money that isn't tied up in RRSPs. A better alternative is to invest the extra company funds by creating a sort of pension fund for the owners..."

Paul nodded his understanding. "I get it—but you know us well enough to know we control personal spending well. We take getting ready for retirement seriously..."

"Indeed, I do! You and Mandy understand having a system worked out in advance is useful. Yes, some of my clients—such as medical doctors—really don't need the money to finance expansion. Often, I suggested they transfer a standard, monthly amount to their personal bank account. By doing so, they invested excess funds regularly, and those funds transformed into their retirement fund." Dan shook his head. "But, again—this type of plan requires a lot of discipline..."

Just then, Mandy and Harry appeared at the door of Dan's office. "Hey, you two—you've been at it for quite a while!" She smiled at her husband. "I hope you're learning something," she teased with a grin.

Paul was up in a flash, giving his wife and son a quick kiss. "I am learning!" He looked at his son's sleepy eyes. "You know, if you stay with us for a while, I bet Harry will fall asleep in a heartbeat—besides, I know you have a few questions..."

Chapter Ten—Incorporating a Company

"Sounds like a plan." Mandy made herself comfortable in an overstuffed easy chair, perfect for a sleepy baby. "I remember—although I can't remember when it was—you mentioned you were worried about a big salary because of audit possibilities . . ."

Paul agreed. "You're right, and we just talked about that a few minutes ago . . ."

"Oh—well, it didn't seem a problem if we go the dividend route. At least, that's how I understood it when Paul tried to explain it to me a couple of weeks ago . . ." She glanced at her husband. "That's when you were reading that book on incorporation . . ."

Paul knew exactly what she was talking about—but, he found learning from Dan a much easier task. "When you explain it to me," he told his neighbor, "I understand it better!"

Dan let out a gut laugh. "It's not easy—I've been doing this a long time, and I know what situations can exist. It's just nice to see a young couple so interested in planning their lives . . . "

Mandy glanced at the computer screen, leaning forward just enough to make sure she could read it. "While you have your model open, will you please try something else for us?"

"Sure!" What do you want to know?"

"Well—Paul and I put in a lot of time into his business plan—we actually think he can make more like $300,000 a year. Will the taxes explode?"

"I don't need my model to answer that—here's where the extra $100,000 goes . . ." He pointed at the screen. "Company taxes rise 13.5%, so that's $13,500. The other $86,000 stays in the company to finance expansion. But—remember that's assuming you aren't spending any of that extra profit personally . . ."

"But, what happens," Mandy asked, "if we expand quickly? I'm not too sure there will be any cash to spend. But, just so I know, say we spent $8,000 a month instead of $6,000. Would the personal tax of $2,900 go up much?"

Dan swiveled his chair so he was facing the computer screen. "For that, I need the model! Let's look . . . " After a few moments, he had the answer. "Personal taxes jump to about $8,700 . . ."

"Holy cow! They triple?" Mandy was shocked!

"Yep—they triple. Once you start paying taxes on dividends, the tax rises pretty quickly. Remember—it's like you paid the first 13.5% of your taxes because the company paid it for you. In the second bracket—where you would be—the personal rate is 30.5% on extra money you make. I had to increase your dividends by $31,000 to give you the extra money you wanted, as well as pay the extra personal taxes." He paused to let his findings sink in. "So—30.5% less 13.5% is 17%. The $30,000 times 17% is $5,100 and that's about what your taxes went up. Of course, if you take out a big lump, it gets a lot worse since you rise into higher brackets . . ."

Mandy glanced at Harry who was snoring softly. "So—continuing to be frugal is the key for keeping our total taxes down?"

"That's about the size of it . . . the government is allowing you to put off a big portion of your taxes because they know small businesses employ most Canadians. They know small businesses need cash to grow, and this is how they help you. But, if you start buying sailboats—like me—the government collects the old tax you owe."

Chapter Ten—Incorporating a Company

Paul glanced at his wife. "I suppose that seems fair—we end up paying the same tax in the long run, right?"

"Maybe—it depends on whether tax rates go up or down in the future. The current rates are really good—in fact, Canada is almost seen as a tax shelter by other countries." He paused as Harry made a few snorting noises. "That's a nice change from a few years ago—so, I suppose the only concern is if future rates are higher, you may pay more later than you could pay now. One common plan is to use the lower brackets up by paying more dividends than you really need . . ."

"Wait—what?" Mandy had a slightly glazed look in her eyes, which Dan attributed to being tired.

"What happens is the money you don't take out becomes a loan from you to the company. Years later—if you do take out a lump for something like a home renovation—you can record that withdrawal as a collection of the loan instead of paying dividends in one of the higher brackets. But, I imagine if you started a company, cash would be so valuable to you that paying any taxes beyond the bare minimum would be foolish . . ."

"But, what if the company is just investing the money instead of expanding and employing more people?" Paul asked. "Wouldn't the government want to collect the old tax we haven't paid?"

Dan nodded. "Luckily, they don't collect the old tax until you take the funds out of the company . . ."

Paul and Mandy looked at each other, then at Harry, and Dan understood perfectly.

"You two get out of here—you need your beauty sleep!"

Chapter Eleven

Eligible Dividends

The day finally came—Harry was about to have a little brother or sister. And, although the news sparked a happy celebration with family and friends, Paul and Mandy started to feel a bit of a strain as the second trimester rolled around. Mandy knew how difficult it was to take care of one child, but two? She also knew if they were to create their own plumbing company, Paul wouldn't be around much to help carry the load—he would have enough to do. But, before bringing their little bundle of joy into the world, Mandy was in the position of having to keep her feet up—bed rest, if she weren't careful. Taking time to follow doctor's orders did one thing for her, however—it gave her time to research information about starting their own company. Even though she respected Dan's information, she figured she could learn more if she spent some quality time on Google.

She was interested in dividends since they were likely how she and Paul would be paid once they owned their own company. Of particular interest was an article that popped up during an Internet search talking about paying no personal tax if all a person had for income was $52,000 of dividends. But, when she thought about what Dan told Paul and her about their paying about $1,500 on dividends of under $40,000—well, it's safe to say Mandy was confused.

"Hey—what do you think about my talking to Dan again about dividends?" She eyed her husband as he spread peanut butter and jelly on a piece of bread for Harry.

"Great idea!" Paul licked the tip of the knife. "With my working side jobs plus my regular job, I don't have a lot of time—you can tell me what you learn." Paul glanced at his wife. "Are you sure you're up for it?"

Mandy smiled at her husband's concern. "I'm not an invalid, Paul! I figure I'll ask Dan to come over during Harry's nap time—that should give us plenty of time . . ."

"Well, I'm all for it—I heard some banging a few minutes ago, and I think he's fixing his mailbox—do you want me to ask him?"

Mandy nodded and, an hour later, Dan made himself comfortable in Paul's favorite chair in the den. "So—Paul tells me you're researching dividends, and you're a little confused. How can I help?"

Mandy recounted the information in the Internet article, ultimately confessing none of it made sense to her.

Dan laughed. "I don't blame you! It can get confusing!" He reached for his laptop. "I never thought I'd be carrying around one of these," he admitted as he fired it up. A few minutes later, his program was up, ready to go. "Okay—let's

Chapter Eleven—Eligible Dividends

play with my model, and I'll see if I can figure out what the article refers to . . ."

Dan scanned the article, adjusting his glasses as he tilted the laptop screen back a little. "Ah! Look . . ." He changed his seating to the couch next to Mandy. "If you had $52,000 of eligible dividends, the tax is only $107. That must be it—but with your small business, you would receive ineligible dividends. Not eligible . . ."

Mandy still didn't get it. "So—I'm assuming there's some logic to this?"

"Remember—the personal tax on dividends is lower because the government recognizes the tax your company already paid. The tax on a small business is extremely low because the government wants to give you the ability to grow your company, as well as employ more people."

"So, let me guess—big businesses pay a higher rate of tax. If the company pays more, then the personal tax is less so the total tax is fair." Mandy cocked an eyebrow as she tried to understand. "I'm guessing," she continued, "when a company only pays the low tax, it's ineligible for a good deal—that's why they call it an ineligible dividend." A quick glance at Dan confirmed her statement. "But, if a company pays the big tax rate, it's eligible for a better deal . . ."

Dan offered a high five. "Nice! That's a terrific guess, and you're exactly right. For example, in Alberta, the small business rate is 13.5% on the first $500,000 of active business income. But, on income above $500,000 the rate rises to 27%."

"Only 27%? So—if Paul and I had a company and made 1.5 million, we would pay $67,500 on the first $500,000 and $270,000 on the next million. Overall, that's only about 23% tax . . ." Mandy thought about that for a moment. "That sounds reasonable—although, I can't imagine writing a cheque for $320,000. But, it's still a great rate!" She laughed at the idea of writing a check that huge.

"I think so, too—these are about the lowest tax rates I've seen in my forty-year career..."

"Is it because we're in Alberta?"

Dan shook his head. "Not really—generally, corporate tax rates are similar across Canada. Ontario is a bit higher than the Western Provinces, and Quebec and the Maritimes are a bit higher than Ontario. But, for the most part, it's all pretty competitive..."

"No Alberta advantage?

"Yes, but not on income tax —the big advantage we all enjoy is because we have no provincial sales tax. Just the Federal GST of 5%..."

Mandy shifted her weight to get more comfortable. "Right—anyway, getting back to dividends for a minute, if the Alberta corporate rate on small business is 13.5%, and 27% on big business, then my personal tax on dividends should be 17% more if it comes from a small business... right?"

Dan nodded. "Sort of—so, let's say you're in a 30.5% personal tax bracket. That would be true if you had $50,000 of interest income—you'll pay about $9,500 income tax on that $50,000. Now, say a company you own made $10,000. Ignoring CPP for a minute, if you earned that personally, you would pay $3,200 in addition to the $9,200." He paused to make sure she was still with him. She was. "But, because it was income earned inside your small business corporation, you only pay $1,350." Again, Dan paused. "However, if you paid out the $8,650 that's left over as a dividend to yourself,

Chapter Eleven—Eligible Dividends

you would think you should owe $3,050 less the $1,350 which is $1,700. Right?" He waited for Mandy to confirm her understanding. "When I use my model, it's actually $1,710—not perfect, but close . . ."

While Dan reviewed the numbers, it was a good time to check on Harry, and grab a quick snack. Once situated again on the couch, she popped a chocolate into her mouth. "Okay—so if it were a big business earning the $10,000, the company tax is $2,700. That means my dividend can only be $7,300 because that's what remains . . ." Mandy paused, realizing her numbers may not be accurate. "So—what I should owe is $3,050 less $2,700. Or, $350?"

"That's right—but let's put that in my model and see what it is actually is." A few clicks on the keyboard, and the numbers filled in. "Yep—it's actually $552. Again, very close." He waited for Mandy to digest the numbers on the screen. "Anyway, you can see the tax on the eligible dividend—in this case—is about 30% of the tax on the ineligible dividend. But, it's all about adjusting for the extra tax your company paid . . . make sense?"

Mandy nodded. "Yes—but something you said earlier is confusing me. When we talked about the information I found on the Internet, you said I would owe almost nothing on dividends from a big business of $52,000? But, on only $7,300, I owe $350 . . ."

"Remember, however, you can't have other types of income—just dividends. In this example, we assume you have $50,000 of interest income. Normally, people have a variety of income with only a small portion being dividends—the big exception is people who own their own company like you and Paul in the future."

Mandy glanced at her neighbor. "So—I guess the tax is lower because if it's all dividends, we're using up the lower brackets..."

"That's correct—and remember on the first $15,000 or so, there's only something like a $500 of tax. Technically, that isn't really a tax bracket—it's using up your non-refundable credits." Dan paused, and looked at his watch. "I gotta get out of here—anyway, the company pays tax on the first dollar it earns, so it's really comparing the total tax either way." He watched as Mandy unwrapped a second chocolate. "Sorry it's so complicated..."

Mandy laughed. "I can't believe I didn't think to record our conversation! How on earth am I going to remember what to tell Paul?"

Dan laughed as he opened the door. "The good news is I live right next door—let me know if you need a refresher course!"

****

Things didn't slow down for Paul. With his regular job plus side jobs, again he felt as if he weren't chipping in as much as he should when it came to Mandy and Harry. And, with Mandy's being pregnant—well, although he was thrilled, he had to admit it threw a slight wrench into things.

Of course, Mandy was her usual-trooper self, and she rarely complained. The doc wound up putting her on bed

Chapter Eleven—Eligible Dividends

rest for the duration of her pregnancy, and it was a day for celebration when she and Paul brought Maggie home. Things couldn't have been more perfect—a young family of four with the world at their feet, and Paul and Mandy began planning for their future in earnest. During the course of Mandy's pregnancy, they had plenty of time to review all the information Dan gave them, as well as what he explained to Mandy a few months before Maggie came into the world.

The first thing they had to do was prioritize.

A week after Maggie's arrival, Dan and Linda stopped by to meet her. "She's gorgeous!" Linda exclaimed as she realized how much the baby looked like Mandy.

"I'll say! She's the spittin' image of her mother!" Dan gently touched Maggie's tiny fingers as they curled into a loose fist.

Paul and Mandy beamed. And, why wouldn't they?

"There's one more thing," Paul announced.

Dan and Linda raised their eyebrows at the same time. "Well?"

"Mandy and I decided we're going to start seriously planning the opening of our new business—we spent time thinking and learning about it, but unless we decide to do it, our own business will always be a dream and in the planning stage . . ."

"Congratulations!" Dan enthusiastically shook Paul's hand, and gave Mandy a quick peck on the cheek.

"Thanks—but, to be honest, I'm afraid I'll mess up how to plan everything . . ." He flashed a huge grin at his friend. "You know I'll be coming to you for advice!"

"You better! You're lucky you have me next door—almost everyone needs advice and help and, down the road, you'll likely use a good public accounting firm to help you with necessary decisions . . ." He paused when Maggie curled her fist around his finger. "My only caution is this—make sure your advisor understands the need for keeping the money inside the company. Otherwise, you could end up on salaries and have your savings stuck in CPP and RRSPs." He glanced at Paul. "That might be fine when your company is no longer growing, but not when you need the money to internally finance growth . . ."

Paul nodded. "One thing—I heard a guy say he got a tax-free dividend. Is that possible?"

"Yep—generally it relates to when a company has a capital gain. But you know that's pretty unlikely when you're getting a plumbing company going. I think if we talked about this, we would be way ahead of what is relevant to you. So let's not confuse things for now . . ."

Just then Maggie sputtered, letting Mandy know it was time for the dinner bell.

Paul grinned with all the pride of a new father. "Right—my head is already spinning!"

Chapter Twelve

Small Businesses
(a great place for a return!)

It was several weeks before Paul and Dan could get together again. With Paul's becoming a father for the second time, he spent more time away from home, picking up extra side jobs, and doing so came as no surprise—the young couple planned for it, and Mandy became a pro at motherhood without her better half at her side. It was a situation bothering Paul, but, what could he do? Raising another child was a pricey proposition, and he had to prepare for the unexpected. So, it became a 'make hay while the sun shines' situation, and they didn't complain—Paul and Mandy still planned a date night each week, both welcoming time together without the kids. They talked about the future, how much it would cost to raise the children as well as start a plumbing business—but they refused to be dissuaded.

Three months after bringing Maggie home, Dan and

Paul finally had time to talk about a few things that were troubling him about starting their new business. So, they left the girls to their own devices, meeting at their favorite local coffee shop on a Saturday morning.

Both men settled into their seats, taking a well-deserved drink of their lattes. "I've always been a straight coffee guy, but ever since Mandy got me hooked on these babies, I'll order a latte every time!" Paul laughed, wiping a bit of cream from his lips. "So—here we are. You know, of course, I'm plying you with coffee so you'll feel obligated to tell me everything you know about starting a small business..."

Dan let out an infectious belly laugh. "Oh, I get it! Well, what is it you want to know?"

Paul grinned. "If it makes you feel any better, the lattes are on me..." He paused for a second, as if gathering his thoughts about what he wanted to say. "You might not remember, but, a long time ago, you really blew my mind talking about a 24% return while owning a plumbing company..."

"I recall the conversation..."

"Well, I've been a plumber for a long time, and I never heard of people investing in plumbing businesses—or, plumbers borrowing at 24%. But the comment really stuck in my brain—do you remember?"

"I do—but, I think at the time, I was making an off-the-cuff comment. That said, I do know what you're talking about—and, it could be important to you if you decide to buy an existing plumbing company..."

"That's what I want to know..."

Dan nodded, took a drink, and settled into the back of his chair. "Small and medium-sized businesses," he began, "are like anything else—the price is dependent on supply and demand. Generally, prices are low because supply far exceeds demand. That's been true for a long time, but especially today with the baby boomers trying to retire."

"I'm not sure I get it—maybe you should start with the basics..."

Dan looked at his young friend knowing how difficult it was to understand the ins and outs of starting a small business. "Sorry—I was getting ahead of myself. Let's talk about how a small or medium-sized business is normally valued."

"That's good—and go slowly!"

"I will—the basic principle is this: if you have a $1,000,000 GIC and it pays say 2% interest, then it follows the income is $20,000 per year. But, for example's sake, let's say you only knew the income was $20,000, and the rate was 2%. With those two facets alone, you can calculate the value of the GIC." He paused. "The high school math is $20,000 divided by 0.02—or, to make it easier, let's use multiplying instead of dividing by a small number."

"What do you mean?"

"Just this—1 divided by the interest rate can give you what is called a multiplier. 1 divided by 0.02 equals a multiplier of 50. That means the simple way to calculate the value of the GIC is 50 times the $20,000 income equals one million. For every interest rate there is a multiple—for 25% it's 4. For 5% it is 20..."

"I'm still not sure how that's going to come into play..."

Dan nodded. "When we're valuing a business, we need two things—the income and the multiplier. So, let's say the business income is $100,000—if we want a return of 25%, the multiplier is 4. Yes, it's simplistic, but the value of the business can be calculated by 4 times $100,000—or, $400,000."

"That's simple..."

"Indeed. But remember—the devil is in the details."

"I took accounting in high school—don't you just get the income from the income statement?"

Dan shook his head. "There's a lot more to it—the income statement numbers from the last few years are certainly a starting point, but you need to fix the numbers so they will better reflect the future. After all—it's the future income you're buying, not the past." Dan could see Paul was struggling to understand the concepts. "Sometimes, people talk about EBITA..."

"I heard of that, but I'm not sure what it is..."

"All it means is 'earnings before interest expense, income taxes, and amortization.' You'll often want to ignore interest because that's more about how you finance the business—remember, a $30,000 car is worth $30,000 regardless if there's a car loan, or not. Truthfully, though, income taxes probably shouldn't be ignored entirely because you still have to pay your taxes..."

"How does that relate to my business?"

"The taxes are often influenced by amortization, or what they used to call 'depreciation.' For example—you operate out of a shop building that's rising in value. You can still claim depreciation on the shop for tax purposes..." Dan eyeballed his friend, then the pasty case holding an enticing array of muffins.

Paul noticed. "Are you hungry? The cheese Danish is killer..."

Chapter Twelve—Small Businesses

Dan laughed. "As much as I'd like to, I have to watch my girlish figure! Anyway, EBITA means before any of that stuff—interest, tax, and depreciation are numbers easily manipulated. But, let's get back to basics on something you know well—a plumbing business. The biggest adjustment is what expenses relate to the owner—say his salary is $70,000. But, he deducts another $10,000 in expenses for meals, his wife's car, or whatever may have little to do with the business. The upshot is he's taking $80,000. On the other hand, a good manager of the business—who doesn't own it—might need to make $120,000. So, you need to deduct the missing expense of $40,000 . . ."

Paul looked completely confused. "Wait a minute—are you saying if I bought the business and managed it myself, I should ignore what I pay myself, assuming it's fair?"

"Yep—that's exactly what I'm saying. The concept is you shouldn't have to buy yourself a job. If the business made $200,000 before any salary to you—and, let's assume a fair salary would be $120,000—then you can say the business made another $80,000 over and above the fair salary. But, when you're buying a business, you should only be paying for the extra profit of $80,000. Sometimes, however, people buy a business strictly as an investment, and they employ a manager . . ." He focused on Paul. "Now, does that affect a small plumbing company? Probably not. Either way, though, it's the concept . . ."

"Is that the only adjustment I'll need to make?"

"Nope! Here's another example—let's say you rented the shop for $90,000—but, it was an old lease, and the landlord will soon be getting $110,000. So, if you buy this business in the future, your profit will fall by the $20,000 rent increase. Better adjust for that, too . . ."

"What does that do for the business?"

"All it means is you're buying future cash flow—granted, it's a bit simplistic, but it's good enough for now..."

Both men opted for a quick restroom and muffin break before they continued their conversation. Paul wasn't sure he understood it all, but he got the gist of how to make the most out of opening a small business. "So," he commented, "the business I'm working for pays the owner a fair salary, and the business makes—on top of that salary—a cash flow fixed by whatever adjustments, and it works out to . . . $200,000 a year. You mentioned a multiplier of 4, so I would pay $800,000—right? It's as simple as that?"

"Kind of—you're getting the basic concept, but these are huge transactions, and you'll need expert help. Not to mention, there's a lot more to it than saying the multiplier is 4—however, it's unlikely to be less than 2, or greater than 5. It's all about negotiation, and you have to make sure you know what you're buying..."

Paul shook his head. "Geez! Using 2, the price is $400,000 and, at 5, it's $1,000,000! That doesn't make sense to me—in our company, all the equipment, the value of uncompleted jobs, and accounts receivable would be a pretty big number. Why would the owner sell for less than he would get by finishing the work, collecting the receivables, and selling the equipment?"

"You're right—that would sort of be the floor price. Let's say all this stuff added up to $700,000—and, let's stick with the adjusted income of $200,000 using the 4 times multiple. That's $800,000. So, the total price exceeds the floor price by $100,000—it's sort of a bonus the seller is getting because he gets good profits." Dan took a moment while Paul digested his information. "The business lingo for this is 'goodwill.' It's obviously the dangerous part of the price because we can't point to anything solid—it's intangible."

Chapter Twelve—Small Businesses

"I thought goodwill was about customer service..."

"It is, but there's more to it. You need to figure out why the goodwill exists—for instance, the goodwill is there because the customers know and love the owner—but he's retiring. In that case, the goodwill could be personal, and may evaporate when the owner retires. Or, maybe the goodwill is there because you have the only business in that part of town—goodwill due to location. But what if someone moves in?" From Paul's reaction, Dan knew that was a possibility to which Paul hadn't given much thought. "It isn't enough to see there is a calculated number—you need to determine if profits will stay high in the future..."

"Okay—let me see if I have this right. If the goodwill number was low, I could use a bigger multiplier—then the goodwill number gets bigger..."

Dan grinned at his friend. "That's right—the multiplier is determined by taking risk and growth into account. If the business has huge potential to grow, the multiplier can head upward. Think of it this way—if earnings bounce around like crazy depending completely on the skill of the manager as well as the luck in getting good work, why would you pay much more than just the tangible assets?"

As much as he would have loved to grasp Dan's information on the first go 'round, it wasn't happening. "Something doesn't make sense to me—why would someone sell for such a cheap price? Instead of selling, couldn't they continue to operate for four years? They'd get the same money, and still own the business..."

"You catch on fast! Yes—many people reach the same conclusion. For the sake of example, let's say they are sixty-one, and have 5 million outside the business in savings. If they're still having fun, maybe they should keep going—but, what about five or ten years later? It's likely they'll feel they want to pack it in regardless if the price is low . . .'"

"Why is that?"

"Because they probably have all the money they could ever spend—so, they may sell it on the open market, but sometimes, they'll sell it to a sharp young person or group of people already working for them. There is also a danger they'll wait until there is a crisis of some sort—health, for example. However, such an unplanned event is a lousy way to deal with the issue—still, there may be things the owner needs to do before they sell. For example, there may be key procedures needing to be followed, but those procedures aren't in writing . . ."

"What about my own goodwill?"

"Not sure what you mean . . ."

Paul hesitated, trying to organize his thoughts. "Well, the guy I work for put me in charge of doing plumbing for dentists—it's tricky work and, most of the time, the work is on weekends. I have to make sure the dentist is back in business on Monday, or there's hell to pay. But, the good news is I'm beginning to build a name for myself with the dentists as well as the contractors they use. Isn't that worth something?"

Dan nodded, and polished off the last of his muffin. "You bet—in cases like that, you might start your own business one day. Or, maybe the owner will sell his business to you and give you a terrific deal. Part of the reason you might get a good deal is because he recognizes the part of the goodwill you created . . ."

Paul was finally starting to understand, but, as you can imagine, he still had questions. "I get it—I think. But, while buying a valuable business can be a great investment, I can't see how someone like me can save up for something so huge. Can't I go to a bank and get a loan? It seems a lot easier . . ."

Dan shook his head. "Not likely, especially when there is a lot of goodwill. Sometimes, the seller will provide some of the financing, but he has to trust you if he's getting less up front than he could by liquidating. To illustrate, say the business assets are worth 4 million, but there's also 1 million of goodwill . . ." Dan paused to let the scenario sink in. "But," he continued, let's say all you can get from the bank is 3 million, and you want the owner to carry the other 2 million. In such an example, he's only seeing 3 million immediately—and maybe he'll never get anything more if the purchaser messes up. Maybe the seller would be more comfortable just getting the sure 4 million by liquidating . . ."

Paul's expression said everything Dan needed to know. It was a lot for the young man to take in. "There's so much to learn," he said.

"You're right—there is, but, luckily, since you're a young guy, you have a lot of time . . ." Trust me—you don't want to buy a business before you're ready. That's why many people fail . . ."

****

So, what do you think? Overall, you can probably see how challenging the whole thing is. Sellers are reluctant to sell because prices are so low, but prices are low because there are few qualified buyers—those who have the money and the talent to operate the business—and huge companies or investment groups such as pensions aren't typically interested until the business is worth at least 10 million. Really tiny businesses often sell because people want to be in business—but, once the business is worth around 2 million, many can't afford them, or finance them.

Then there's this—to make matters worse, potential sellers have few people they can turn to for help. It's a tough business to be in because, usually, people know little about it. "I can't tell you how many times I chatted with client about the challenges of getting anything like what seems to be a fair price," Dan told Paul. "It's tough to send someone a bill when the best decision is to continue on with running the business. If that were all I did, I sure wouldn't have had much of a practice..."

Dan went on to tell Paul there are some business brokers around who will just take listings—but that's pretty dangerous. Think about it—if you found out the business you worked for were for sale, wouldn't you think about working for someone else? Of course, you would—but, some of the bigger public accounting firms help bigger businesses sell, but, typically, they want to see the business is worth 5 million or more. And, they often charge good-sized fees up front—$50,000 or more regardless of whether or not the business sells.

What should you take away from this conversation? Just this—overall, it's a lot easier to sell a 2 million dollar piece of real estate than a 2 million dollar business.

Chapter Thirteen

Time to Own

Paul turned thirty that year. The kids were growing like weeds, Mandy plucked out a grey hair or two, and during introspective moments—when he had a solid minute or two to himself—he questioned whether he and Mandy were making the right decision about opening their own plumbing business. Were they doing the right thing? Were the risks too great? What if they failed? As you can imagine, the decision to take the plunge didn't come easily for the young couple. In fact, they agonized over it—but, when they finally decided to go for it, there was a thrill they could barely explain!

Of course, there was a celebration backyard barbecue as he entered his thirties, and somewhere during grilled chicken and corn on the cob Paul confessed to Dan he felt a little weird about such a milestone birthday. Up until then, he felt young and motivated—turning thirty, however, meant life was getting serious.

As it turned out, Dan felt the same way when he turned thirty, and he confessed it was the only birthday that really bothered him. In a strange way, he felt disconnected—he wanted to get things going. He wanted to kick his career into high gear.

He wanted success.

So, in many ways, Paul and Dan were alike—yes, they were a generation apart, and passing time came with plenty of changes. Still, when it came right down to it, Paul and Dan were really no different. But, as the calendar turned, Paul had a new feeling—people trusted him. They trusted him as a preferred authority in his chosen field, as well as his ability to complete any plumbing challenge—and, complete it well. Side jobs helped, but most of his experience came from his boss's trusting him with the task of estimating and keeping tough jobs running efficiently, and cost effectively.

"The interesting thing," Paul told Dan, "is Nick's being around less and less, and I think he's ready to turn it over to me . . ." The bad thing was Paul wasn't too sure what that meant, or when it might happen—and that made him feel up in the air. He was getting impatient, and Nick's not taking action only served to amp up Paul's considering going out on his own.

It was a point of view Dan understood, but, as usual, he believed there was much more to it, and he presented the issue to Paul from Nick's point of view. "If I were Nick," he commented, "I would be wondering if you're loyal to me, and whether you want to take over. I certainly would have to consider the possibility of your talking to other plumbing companies—or, starting your own business. In both cases, I would be nervous you might try to take my customers . . ."

Chapter Thirteen—Time to Own

Dan went on to further suggest Paul's giving Nick the succession plan he seemed to need. "For a couple your age," he said, "it's pretty impressive you're getting close to having no mortgage. Frankly, though, you don't have the money to buy Nick's company, and Nick must be willing to carry you or the deal isn't going to happen. On the other hand, you need to be sure this is what you and Mandy want. I imagine—if you fail—it won't be pretty. Odds are Nick would get the business back, and you guys would lose your home . . ."

Well—you can imagine what a sobering thought that was! But, Paul refused to be dissuaded. From day one, he and Mandy aways kept failure—stemming from whatever reason—at the forefront of their minds. They figured if they pushed it too far back, they could become complacent. Both knew opening their own business would be a giant risk and, hopefully, it would be the only big risk they would have to take. Doing so was critical to their future as a family . . .

But, as Dan explained, Paul and Mandy had to look at the flip side—did Nick understand the worth of his business? Dan and Paul had many conversations about how business owners often don't know the real numbers—a price of three to five years of profit sounds too low to many of them. And, as they discussed, profit excludes a fair salary for their efforts. That's not all—the total price includes everything Paul needs to run the business, such as equipment and accounts receivable.

Knowing Paul as well as he did by then, Dan knew Paul learned best by having an example. "Let's guess," he began, "a fair price for Nick's business is $1,000,000, and the tangible assets are worth $700,000—that means the goodwill is only $300,000. Realize, of course, Nick could get $700,000—risk free—by winding down. By selling to you and carrying the debt, he only gets an additional $300,000—but, he also takes on the big risk of your not paying him . . ."

It didn't take Paul long to grasp Nick needed to like and trust him in order to offer Paul the opportunity to own his own business. Nick had to know Paul was fully committed, talented, and trustworthy. Dan went on to say if he were in Nick's shoes thinking about taking such a risk, he'd up the price of goodwill to $400,000 . . . just as a bit of insurance.

Clearly, it was something to think about, but his question was how long would he owe Nick. Dan said his rule of thumb was to maintain existing income, and use the excess to pay off the owner in about five years. "So, in a deal like yours," he said, "your income, before tax, needs to increase by about $250,000. I know that totals $1,250,000—but remember you will likely be paying something like 5% interest. You'll need to pay corporate tax of about 14% . . ."

"But, I guess after that five years," Paul commented, "my income will be wonderful in terms of living better and being able to save for retirement. And frankly, I think I can increase the company's profit a bit—I'm more than willing to work long hours, and I think I can increase prices without losing customers. Maybe I can pay him off quicker . . ."

As Dan listened to his protégé, he couldn't help but feel the pride a father often feels for his son. Even though their friendship wasn't a decade old, Dan couldn't help but think Paul would be a great success—but, only if he made intelligent decisions. He went on to tell Paul if Nick were prepared to charge a fair market price as well as carry him—well, why wouldn't he want the deal?

"One thing Nick will be thinking of," Dan offered, "is what happens if you go elsewhere. If he's sincere about retirement, losing you would be a big mess because he would have to sell on the open market. And, odds are the business isn't really ready to be sold to an outsider . . ."

It was obvious Nick would most likely prefer to sell to

Paul. After all, he knew how things were done as well as the customers. If Nick were smart, he'd also be thinking about what he had to lose—staff, customers, and retirement. Think about what would happen to Nick's business if word got out regarding his selling—goodbye customers, hello hassle!

All the talk about what a good position Paul might be in as Nick considered selling made Paul wonder if Nick needed him that badly, why shouldn't he ask for a discounted price? All of his hard work over the last several years certainly placed him in a position of power, so why shouldn't he take advantage of it?

Dan knew why. "Frankly, if he's prepared to carry you, also asking for a reduced price is seeking a lot—it looks greedy. Don't forget—initially he collects a lot less than he would get from simply winding down. From what you told me, Nick is a nice guy and a good businessman, so there's the possibility he might decide to be nice to you—so don't negotiate too hard. I assure you, Nick will know you need this deal a lot more than he . . ."

"There's another thing," Paul offered. "Nick owns the building—his businesses uses two bays, and he rents out the other eight—what about talking to him about buying the building?"

"I wouldn't—but you'll have to deal with the issue of rent. A reasonable rent should be factored into the calculation of profit, and you'll be paying Nick as your landlord. I imagine you'll end up with something like a five-year lease—I wouldn't tie yourself to the building too long. Who knows? In five years you might want to buy the building, or you might outgrow that location. Right now, I'd concentrate on the plumbing business, and not try to own commercial real estate at the same time. Getting too aggressive can really come back to bite you . . ."

Everything Dan said made sense, but Paul still was a little uneasy about knowing the right decision to make. "What do you suggest I do," he asked, hoping Dan could point him in the right direction.

"I'd talk to Nick, letting him know you wish to buy the business—see what he has to say. When negotiating, you're always better off when you learn what the other guy wants. Who knows? Maybe what he wants is better than what I guessed! Either way, I think you'll know quickly if he's serious as well as prepared to be reasonable . . ."

Paul was quiet for a couple of minutes as he thought about what lay in front of him. "Well—wish me luck," he said, shaking Dan's hand.

But, Dan had one more bit of advice. "If it seems a deal is likely, let Nick know I'll be happy to meet with his accountant. If this deal happens, it has to be a 'friendly' deal—getting lawyers involved too soon can kill this kind of transaction. Let's just try to reach an understanding first . . ."

Paul sighed with relief.

Dan was in his corner . . .

Chapter Fourteen

The Conversation

It's always a difficult thing—change, I mean. When Paul and Mandy decided to take the plunge (pardon the pun) by opening their own plumbing company, even though Paul knew his boss well, there was still a considerable amount of trepidation. Would Nick think he was nuts? There was always that possibility—but, Paul believed Nick would treat him as he would anyone who wanted to buy his business. Nonetheless, nerves encouraged him to opt for a light breakfast of a bagel and cup of coffee the morning of their meeting.

Paul purposely requested a time to meet for midmorning—plumbers would be out on jobs, and Nick would be in his office. He didn't tell Nick outright what he wanted to discuss, but it probably wasn't difficult to figure out. As he knocked on his boss's door, his mind flipped to Mandy and the kids. *I know this is the right thing to do*, he thought as he took a seat across from him.

Nick tossed a pencil onto his desk, sitting back so he could get a good look at his star employee. He knew, of course, why Paul wanted to talk—it was no secret he wanted to have his own business someday.

A quick swipe of his palms on his pants, Paul took the lead. "Thanks for seeing me—I appreciate it, knowing it was a bit on short notice . . ." Paul paused as if trying to assess what his boss was thinking. "As I mentioned yesterday, Mandy and I feel we have learned enough to run our own plumbing company—she worked at accounting the last few years and, of course, you know the role I have with you . . ."

"You've done an excellent job for me, that's for sure," Nick commented.

"Thanks—you taught me a lot! There's one thing, though—you mentioned a few times you would like to move permanently to Vancouver Island, and you're about ready to turn things over to me . . ." Again, he paused. He rehearsed what he was going to say a million times, but, at the moment, he could remember nothing. "Please know if you give Mandy and me a chance to make that happen for you, we will be totally committed, and we're even prepared to sell our house to raise as much as we can . . ." Paul stopped to take a sip of water. "Anyway—I'm wondering if what I'm proposing is what you want to do. I know it's a big decision . . ."

Nick held Paul's gaze, then smiled. "Well, Paul—I do think we can make a deal . . ."

Paul's eyes lit up!

"I do think you and I are ready for this next phase of life, and the fact is I worry little when I leave you in charge. You're excellent with customers and staff, and you made good suggestions over the last few years. Frankly I don't know what I would do without you . . ."

Chapter Fourteen—The Conversation

"Thank you—that means a lot, and I appreciate your confidence in me..."

"I met with my CPA yesterday," Nick continued, "and we put something together I think will please you. Joe believes I should ask for a bit more, but I'm in good shape financially, and I just want a smooth transition. But, I want to make something clear—I have no intention of entering into a negotiation. Today, I want to be sure you understand what I'm willing to do—after you review the parameters of the sale, you should go home and discuss it with Mandy and your neighbor. I can't remember his name..."

"Dan—the financial planning guy..."

"That's it! Anyway, talk to other advisors if you wish. I'll be happy to answer any questions—I just don't want to negotiate. Joe and I feel this deal is structured to be easy for you, and I think you'll agree the price is fair. But—the key is the terms I'm giving you, and, by that I mean I'm prepared to carry you at a reasonable interest rate. I don't want you to sell your house, but I do appreciate how committed you are..."

Paul was stunned! Even though he hadn't seen a formal proposal, he couldn't believe the opportunity in front of him! "Holy cow! Should I take a few notes?"

"Notes are always a good idea..."

Paul grabbed a pencil from the cup on Nick's desk, and flipped open a small, spiral notepad.

"The first thing to get out of the way is I intend to sell you assets—not shares."

"I'm not surprised—Dan told me it's likely what you would want..."

"Right—both ways of doing a deal have advantages, but selling you my shares would be a huge hassle for me. As you know, I have all of my commercial real estate and investments in the company. Moving them out without paying a bunch of income tax would be really tough . . ."

"Can't your accountants and lawyers make it easier?"

"Yes, but they aren't cheap . . ."

Paul scribbled notes as Nick continued. "Obviously," he said, "you'll want the company name, but that's easy to do. Legal contracts are much harder to transfer, so I suggest any working contracts right now will be finished off in my company. Anything new goes to your new company—and, whenever the customer is willing, we'll move pending jobs to your new company."

"Sounds good to me . . ."

"Similarly, I suggest my company collect outstanding receivables so we don't have to guess on valuation, or make adjustments later. That means you'll be buying the tools, trucks, and goodwill. And, of course, you'll need some working capital as well because, as you know, cash goes out well before it comes in . . ."

"So far, it sounds great—but isn't there tax involved in selling me the operating assets?"

Nick grinned. "Not really—I'm prepared to sell you the equipment for its depreciated amount. The truck and tools get pretty beat up, so I think that's pretty close to what they're worth . . ."

"What about goodwill?"

"Since there is no cost, what I charge you for goodwill is all profit—and, the tax is minimal. Half the sales price

Chapter Fourteen—The Conversation

goes into the capital dividend account, so I can pay myself tax-free dividends from that account. The other half is only taxed at business rates . . ." Nick hesitated, making sure his young employee was keeping up with him. So far, so good. "My year end is coming up," he continued, "and, by finalizing the deal on the first day of my next year, my total business income including the sale of goodwill will be taxed at the low rate—13.5% in Alberta."

"That's all?"

"Yep— here's how ridiculously cheap it is. Say I charge you one million for goodwill—just to keep the math simple. The $500,000 tax-free dividend saves me about $150,000 because, if I took out a normal dividend, that's about what I would pay. I'm thinking of upgrading my sailboat, so this is perfect timing. So, I'll owe 13.5% on the other $500,000—my company cuts a cheque for $67,500. Obviously, I'll pay more tax one day when I take out the $432,500 that's left in the company. But, who cares? That's a long way off . . ."

Paul clicked his pencil for more lead. "So, taxes are actually a negative in the short run?"

"I know it's unbelievable—anyway, don't feel sorry for me because I sold you the assets. By the way, when your company buys goodwill, you actually get tax deductions, slowly, over time, as well."

Paul leaned back, confused. "I'm not sure I get it—will you lay it out for me?"

Nick nodded. "Right—I was jumping ahead. The tools and trucks should cost you about $100,000, and you'll need about $200,000 of working capital. Goodwill? I think it's worth about 1 million, but I'm only going to charge you $700,000—so, the total cash needed will be an even 1 million. Of course, if you start your own company, you'll need to spend the $300,000 anyway. Likely more, because there are a bunch of small tools, supplies, and bits of office equipment that were expensed when we bought them—I'm just throwing all of that in . . ."

"Overall, it sounds fair . . ."

Nick studied Paul, and he could see the wheels turning. "So—what do you think you can put down?"

"Mandy and I have a ton of equity in our house, so we should be able to increase the mortgage by at least $100,000. And, my Dad is prepared to lend me $100,000 . . ."

"Okay— that sounds fair. I'm happy to carry the rest . . ."

"What about the rent?"

"We could do up a lease for five years at about what the other tenants are paying. All in, that would be about $5,000 a month. Of course, I would love to keep you as a tenant, but a five-year lease is long enough. You have to do what's best for your business, and you might outgrow my building . . ."

Paul thought for a moment. "When we were looking at the financials the other day, it seems like the income before your salary is about $500,000 a year. So, surely I can make good payments on what I owe you, but I'm a bit worried about working capital. It seems you can never have too much . . ."

Nick nodded his understanding. "I think you'll be okay, but let's do a quick calculation. First, we need to take off the $60,000 rent, but I don't think we need to take off too much for salary since I don't work very hard. Let's take off $40,000 to be safe—that drops the net to $400,000 before tax, or $344,000 after tax. I need my computer to see what you will pay me—and, by the way, I was thinking I'll charge you prime, plus 3%. Today, that's about 6%. But—to help with the cash flow—I was going to say there were no payments for

Chapter Fourteen—The Conversation

the first six months."

Paul grinned. "That sounds great - let's put that in the computer..."

Nick returned the good-humored grin. "Here we go—no payments for six months, but let's see what the payments will be over the next 4.5 years. It would be nice for both of us if the sale were over in 5 years..." He keyed in the numbers and, instantly, the calculation was at their fingertips. "Okay—so the monthly payment is about $17,500 a month, or $210,000 a year. Of course, for the first couple of years, the interest is about $40,000 a year—that will pull the taxes down a bit, but not enough to worry about."

"That leaves me a little elbow room, doesn't it?"

"Indeed—that extra should stay in the bank for cash flow until you're comfortable. If there's still extra, you can either repay your Dad, or pay me off sooner than expected."

Their hour was nearly up, and Paul couldn't wait to tell Mandy about their conversation. "Everything sounds fair," he told Nick, "but, as you mentioned, I need to discuss this with Mandy and Dan—and, I need to sleep on it! But, we're grateful for this opportunity—without your carrying us, I don't think we could pull it off..."

Nick stood, and walked to the door with the young entrepreneur. "Well—I know how difficult it is to sell, and how long it normally takes. So, yes, I'm helping you, but you're really helping me get going on being completely retired. I sure didn't enjoy the winter here last year, and moving sooner rather than later will be great." He shook Paul's hand. "But, let's not get carried away—you need to talk to Mandy and Dan..."

Moments later, Paul stood by himself, and he realized

his palms were still sweating. He promised Nick he would let him know before the week's end, but he knew his answer already—there's no way he wasn't going to accept.

Chapter Fifteen

The Next Conversation

Since he only had until the end of the week to accept or decline Nick's offer, it was imperative Paul get with Dan as quickly as possible. The main thing he needed to know? Was it a good deal?

Paul, of course, wasn't experienced enough to make such a decision without consulting with a professional, and he considered it his good luck Dan lived next door. Although he didn't have much time the evening of his conversation with Nick, he took the extra couple of minutes to drop off his notes before he walked in his own front door. Now, two days later, life graced him again by providing enough time for a serious conversation with Dan over a couple of beers.

"So," Paul began, "what do you think? Did you have time to look over my notes?"

Dan took a swig. "I did—and I have a few questions . . ."

Paul grinned. "I knew you would—fire away!"

"First, your notes say the profit before salary to Nick is about $500,000. I imagine that's before income tax and amortization—and, I can't imagine Nick pays anyone interest."

"Correct..."

"I also noticed you're taking off a bit for Nick's salary, future rent, and income taxes. But—I'm wondering if you're expecting to run the company differently? You mentioned before Nick tends to undercharge..."

Paul nodded. "I think prices can go up a good 5% to 10%—however, Nick has some old friends and, while they're good customers, I'm sure they realize they pay less than the market. The increased price would produce extra profits of around $100,000 a year..."

"Sounds good—just be sensitive to it. Once it gets out you're buying Nick out, I suggest you meet with the bigger customers for a discussion. Maybe take them some sort of small gift for being such loyal, long term customers..."

Dan couldn't help but think of how different Paul was from the day he met him. Life and family took over, and he and Mandy morphed from being a young married couple, to a full-fledged, serious-about-life family. "If you assure them they will continue to get great service," he continued, "a minor bump in price shouldn't be a problem. The fact is you probably know most of them and, if they realize you need to fund buying Nick out, they're likely fine—as long as they feel your new prices don't exceed the market."

Paul exhaled as if he'd been holding his breath for a week. "Good—so what do you think of Nick's offer, in general?"

Dan grinned. "It looks terrific! I understand you think

Chapter Fourteen—The Next Conversation

the tangible assets are fairly priced—the fact you should be able to pay everything off within four years tells me the total price can't be excessive. Really, though, the key is he will carry you—prime and 3% is very fair. Typically, you couldn't finance this, so getting a low interest rate is wonderful . . ."

"You and Nick sound confident . . ."

Dan agreed. "Well, yes—but, Nick and I know you. Lenders will view you as a start-up business with unproven management. As we discussed, businesses fail—most of the time—due to poor management. And, few people are truly cut out to be business owners . . ." He shifted to a more comfortable position. "Anyway—the point is Nick is taking a big risk to make this happen for you. You're a lucky guy!"

Just what Paul wanted to hear! "Of course, I appreciate what Nick is doing—so does Mandy. But, I told her our only realistic option is to start a new business, and keep it very small . . ."

"Tough option—it could be long time before your new company grows to the size of Nick's . . ."

For several moments, Paul considered his friend's words. "There are small tools as well as general supplies, and Nick isn't charging me for them. By comparison, I researched simple things such as desks, chairs, office supplies—you know, the usual stuff for an office . . ."

Dan nodded.

"It's amazing how expensive everything will be—I can try hitting auctions—or, buy used stuff—but who has the time?"

"Let me ask you a question—what would happen to Nick's business if you didn't buy him out?"

It was something Paul thought about, but not recently, or for very long. "There are some young guys who might be ready in a few years, but, frankly, I would rather have them as my key crew chiefs—not competing with them."

"Ah—so a missing asset is the value of some of the personnel..."

"Yep—a lot of our work is pretty specialized. Frankly, if Nick chose to hang in there for a while, it would be almost impossible for me to get any of the specialized work. Many of the contractors know me, but they've known Nick a lot longer. He has a loyal following..."

Dan was quiet for a few moments as he thought through Paul's opportunity. "Well—this is a good discussion because you're paying a lot for goodwill. While it's nice to do a calculation for what goodwill might be, it's equally important to know why the goodwill exists. In the current situation, a lot of the goodwill is Nick..."

"I know—and, Nick is carrying me. Surely he'll provide help—if I need it— to keep those key clients. So, overall, the combination of the specialized work, plus all the tools and trained staff, is appealing to me."

"It's a generous offer, that's for sure—what does Mandy have to say?"

Paul grinned, and took a final swig. "Well—she wants to do this, as well as help in whatever way she can. Nick uses Quickbooks for his internal accounting and, for that reason, she learned to use the software as well as helping with the bookkeeping. She wants to look at doing job costing, so we can see exactly what we make, job by job..."

"Smart move..."

"I know Nick thinks he should be doing a bit better—he

Chapter Fourteen—The Next Conversation

has a rough idea in his head of what he makes per job, but the total is always less—sometimes a lot less."

"Interesting—what's the problem?"

"Well, I think we might not do as well on certain types of jobs. But, right now, we don't know which jobs are the culprits. Nick always resists job costing, saying he's too old to put up with the hassle . . ."

As a retired man himself, Dan knew exactly how Nick felt. For some reason, as we age, we often don't want—or, need—to learn something new. Sometimes, it's easier to do it the old way and, in Nick's case, job costing was a lot of work. It gets tricky with leftover material, returning things, and accounting for everyone's time—but, the reports can be revealing.

And, Dan told Paul just that.

"I'd love to see those reports," Paul agreed. "But, since that isn't going to happen, I'm thrilled Mandy likes the deal—having her support is critical to me. She and I feel this is the one big risk we need to take—if we do, we'll set ourselves up financially for the rest of our lives. That's if it goes well . . ."

The one thing Paul really wanted to know about was Nick's refusal to negotiate. Was that unusual? Dan concurred, in a way, it was—but it also made a lot of sense. Nick was an experienced businessman—his was a fair sales price, and his offer to carry Paul was worth its weight in gold. With those two things on the table, why would he want to go through the brain damage of a lengthy negotiation? Who would? Besides, tough negotiations can often kill friendships, not to mention the expense of lawyers, accountants, and anyone else who should have a say.

That brought Dan to his next point—legal advice. "Are

you planning on having a lawyer review the offer?" he asked.

"Well—I want have a lawyer look at everything, but Nick made it clear my role is to say yes, or no. Right now, I'm pretty sure the answer will be yes . . ."

Dan nodded. "I'm not surprised. By the way—your lawyer will likely advise you to have Nick sign some sort of non-compete agreement.

"How does that work?"

"It's easy to understand—the idea is if Nick changes his mind, doesn't move to the Island, and stays here to compete, you can initiate a claim for damages.

"He pays?"

"It would likely be reducing or eliminating what you owe him for the goodwill . . ."

Paul frowned, and was quiet for a few moments. "I'm not sure I like the sound of that. First, I know Nick wants to retire and move. If he gets really bored he might do small jobs out on Vancouver Island, but that would be no problem. Second, he's showing such trust in me—how do I turn around and say I don't trust him?"

Dan agreed. "Oh, I know—obviously, you need to talk to a lawyer. I'm just giving you a heads up this is going to come up. If it were me, I'd be inclined to tell Nick the lawyer suggested it, and you could tell him you refused to insist on it."

"Make sense to me—I'll discuss it with a lawyer . . ."

"Good—be smart. Find out as much as you can . . ."

Chapter Sixteen

Is 'Risk' Really a Four-letter Word?

The saying is true—time flies. It seemed a long time since Paul's and Dan's first barbecue—the time when they discussed Paul's idea to have his own plumbing company.

Then, in many ways, it seemed like yesterday.

Four years passed, and it probably comes as no surprise Paul's business was successful—he did everything right from the beginning, including his many conversations with Dan about financial planning. They always referred to it as their backyard barbecue financial planning, and Dan laughed when Paul told him he was ready to cook up his financial success.

Of course, the kids were sprouting like crazy—Harry entered preschool, and Maggie wasn't too far behind. Mandy learned how difficult—and, rewarding—raising a family was, but she still found time to take care of the accounting needs for Paul's business. She learned job costing, and doing so turned out to be invaluable to the business's success.

Dan and Paul continued their discussions about financial planning throughout the years, but they didn't get together as much as each would have liked. So, when they had the opportunity to watch the kids while their wives took a bit of time for themselves, both were delighted!

"Where did you go, again?" Paul asked as he handed Dan a freshly brewed cup of coffee.

Dan took a sip. "Hot!" He laughed as he wiped a bit of cream from his lips. "Germany—we flew to Berlin, then home from Munich..."

"That had to be pretty cool—what was it like?"

"It was cool—Germany has a vibrant economy, and the history is fascinating." He looked at Paul. "Enough about me—bring me up to date. I understand things are going very well..."

Paul grinned, obviously proud of his success. "Well, we just paid Nick off a year ahead of schedule, so that's good. I only touch my line of credit a few times a year—and, we're buying equipment that isn't really for plumbing..."

That was a surprise! "How so?"

"On a lot of commercial jobs we use scissorlifts to move material up a few stories. The contractor would rent one, and all the subtrades would chip in for the rent. So, I scoured auctions, and found I could buy used lifts fairly cheap. I now supply most of my job sites with a scissorlift, and the other trades pay me. I break even on cash flow in about six months, and these things last for years..."

Chapter Sixteen—Is 'Risk' Really a Four-letter Word?

"A sensible investment—you won't get a return like that investing . . ." Dan was impressed at the young man's newfound business skills.

"Agreed—but I'm running out of opportunities like that. Pretty soon I should have $500,000 in the bank, and I don't have a clue about investing. My bank is always calling because, at times, I have a lot of cash—they want me to put it into some of their Canadian mutual funds. According to the bank, I should focus on the resource sector—what do you think?"

Dan's coffee cooled enough for his first good sip. "Man—I hardly know where to begin. As you know, I work part time since retirement, managing my own investments as well as having some of my old clients and friends join me. To be honest? It's been quite an eye opener, even for a CPA . . ."

"What do you mean?"

"Just this—in one way, the biggest issue is risk, and that's something you know about. Isn't risk the big reason you make money in your business?"

Paul nodded, but he still wasn't sure where Dan was going.

"The average guy," Dan continued, "would never bid on one of the contracts you take on all the time—so many things can go wrong. The bottom line is if you really mess up, you don't get paid. Worse? The plumbing could fall apart, and you'll get sued. But, you have the knowledge and experience to cope with the risk—so, it's really the risk that provides your ability to make a living. And, I bet you don't worry about it either . . ."

Paul was about to answer when Harry ran up to them with a grasshopper in his hand. After spending a few minutes oohing and ah-ing over his find, they returned to their conversation, watching Harry run to the backyard where Maggie was playing in her sandbox. "Where were we?" Paul asked.

"Risk—you don't even think about it . . . "

"And, that's true—but there are guys working for me who have a lot of experience, but they just can't handle the responsibility . . ."

"So—overall—you deal with risk in a productive way, and there are two reasons for that. You have the right mental wiring, plus the knowledge and experience in one particular type of construction . . ."

"True, but I have to add I don't take on contracts that are too big. Mistakes do happen, and I don't want one mistake to wipe me out. The plumbers' prayer is, 'let my mistakes be little ones' . . ."

Dan chuckled. "You know, don't you, accountants in public practice have the same prayer—anyway, ignoring plumbing for a minute, how do you make risk work for you?"

Paul thought for a moment. "Well, it's like you said—risk can work for people if they're wired right, don't take on anything excessively large, and are knowledgeable about what they're doing . . ."

"Perfect!" Now, let's take that, and apply it to investing."

"When I think about it, I think I'm wired to take on risk."

"Agreed—and that's true of most successful business owners. If anything, the problem is they're too willing to take wild risks—for some reason, guys are way more likely to be excessively aggressive. Female business owners are, generally, more cautious. The ladies may ultimately take the same risk, but they do a lot better job of doing their homework." Dan hesitated. "But, I guess I'm drifting into the second factor—not taking on anything too excessive..."

"What do you consider an excessive investment?"

"Normally, we use a simple rule such as any individual investment shouldn't exceed 5% of your net worth."

Paul's eyebrows shot up. "But, isn't that limiting?"

"Sometimes—for example, let's say you're going to buy the building you presently rent. That puts you far over the 5% rule—and, your plumbing business is far in excess of it, too. The truth is most wealthy people dramatically broke the rule in their younger years—but, as you get older and are trying to preserve your wealth, you want to take smaller risks. Of course, you'll be more comfortable taking risks when you're personally managing something. Yes, the overall risk is still large, but you're surviving the experience due to superior knowledge." Dan paused, his voice taking a serious turn. "But, do be careful—many folks have lost everything because they continued to take huge risks long after it made sense. You might be a highly knowledgeable and experienced manager, but things can go wrong that are beyond your control..."

"Overall," Paul commented, "that makes sense—but I have a question..."

"Shoot..."

Paul collected his thoughts before answering. "I heard guys talking about the stock market because it took a big drop—it seems like everyone is unhappy. Is it the 5% limit on individual stocks, or is it on the stock market, in general?"

Dan smiled at his friend. "Great question! The theory is you diversify by buying different stocks in different industries located in different parts of the world—the ups and downs offset each other. But, here's the scary thing—studies indicate in a downturn, securities are more likely to go down together. Do you recall the third part of your answer?"

"Yep—I said you had to be knowledgeable about what you were doing. But isn't that tricky when it comes to investing? How can I know much about big companies like Microsoft or Coke?"

Dan nodded. You're right—that's an issue. But, let's start with simpler investments—what about your buying those scissorlifts? Sounds like you're getting your money back in six months. That's an amazing return on investment..."

Paul smiled with pride. "Well, I thought it was just an outgrowth of my plumbing business—but I suppose you're right..."

"Here's the interesting thing—people often wind up ignoring opportunities like your scissorlifts." Dan paused as if trying to remember something. "There was a neat book written about fifteen years ago called *One up on Wall Street* that describes how you can easily know something important from your daily life..."

"I'm not sure I understand..."

"Okay—here's a personal example. Back in 1981, I bought one of the first IBM PCs with the new DOS operating system by an unknown company called Microsoft. I knew the new tool was dramatically important—finally, I had enough memory to do something truly useful with a microcomputer! Why didn't I invest?" Dan paused, briefly considering his life if he invested with the fledgling tech company. "If I bought $10,000 of Microsoft when it went public in 1986, it would be worth over 6 million today..."

"Seriously?"

"Oh, yes—so I offer these two cautions. First, if you invest in something that needs your attention, be careful because you only have so much time. Your main business is your big money maker, so don't get too distracted. Second, make sure the value is something you know of yourself. Not something you're hearing from someone else—in other words, avoid the so called 'hot tip.' If a guy on your hockey team says his buddies have the cure for cancer, refuse to get involved—too often, you lose your money on such deals."

Just as Paul was about to respond, Mandy and Linda joined them in the backyard—the signal to wind it up. Paul watched as Mandy gathered the kids for their naps as Linda gave Dan the high sign it was time to go. "Five minutes?" he asked, glancing at Paul.

"Only five minutes—we have to be at the kids' in thirty minutes . . ." Linda laughed, winking at her husband.

"Okay, okay!" Dan grinned, and turned to Paul. "Anyway—before I go, any thoughts about your bank? You said they're recommending a Canadian mutual focusing on the resource sector . . ."

"Right—using the rules we talked about, I think I have the guts to do it. However, this mutual would be Canadian companies in one industry. I should probably look at whether the entire investment is more than 5% of my net worth since these stocks will likely go up and down together . . ."

"Good thinking—I agree."

"I guess the downside is I know nothing about Canadian resource companies, so I definitely shouldn't invest a lot . . ."

"I agree, again—my recommendation is until you know a lot more about public market investing, I'd hold off. Now that I know you're interested in investing, I can get you a lot more material you should learn . . ."

"Back to school for me, eh?"

"Yep—learn everything you can . . .

Chapter Seventeen

The Market—liquidity and Goals

By the time Paul and Mandy reached their fifth anniversary of being business owners—two weeks after Paul's last conversation with Dan—their lives changed significantly. Things were good, and Paul was thinking about investing, but, according to Dan, there was much to consider when thinking about the stock market—especially liquidity and goals. Of course, Paul was intelligently assessing his risk for all investments he was considering, but it was the stock market that seemed the most foreign to him.

The first thing he had to learn was the pros and cons of each of the three ways to invest—himself, alternative, and public. Confused? Paul was, too, so he again asked for Dan's advice—except this time, he offered to pay him. The way he figured it, Dan was a professional and, if he were providing similar advice to anyone other than Paul, he'd be paid a pretty penny.

But, as you can imagine, Dan refused.

"My payment will be your success—besides, by now, I consider you and Mandy family..."

Paul clapped Dan on the shoulder as they headed for Dan's den. "Well, I don't feel right about it, but I understand—Mandy and I appreciate it!"

Each settled in their favorite chairs—yes, Paul was there often enough to claim one—and he couldn't wait to dive in. "So—by do it myself, do you mean, for example, purchasing something like a commercial building?"

Dan nodded. "Yep—in this type of investment, you have very poor liquidity. In other words, it can take months—or even years—to cash in your investment, and that can really mess you up. Think about it—life happens. Also, owning something like this with a partner or two doesn't normally improve the liquidity—in fact, it often makes it worse..."

"I remember when we talked about this—but, not in detail—a few years ago. If I remember, you said having a shotgun clause could help move things along..."

Dan propped his feet up on the ottoman, settling into the back of his chair. "True—but liquidity is still an issue."

"Why?"

"Okay—let's say you and I owned a commercial building together, and I want to sell. You don't. So I have to sell out to you, or I have to buy you out, and then sell the whole building. The point is a lot of time might be needed..."

"Got it—so where does the goal thing come in?"

"It's really an alignment of goals. Alignment refers to whether the investor and management are motivated by the same end result. Both have to be on the same page—obviously, if you own and operate the whole thing, alignment is perfect.

Chapter Seventeen—The Market—Liquidity and Goals

But, having one partner can produce a misalignment." Dan paused waiting for Paul to catch up with his notes. When Paul looked up, it was the cue to keep going. "So, again, let's say you and I own a commercial building—I may be happy with operating the building, and having the nice yearly rental income. But, you may want to sell as soon as there is appreciation. Here's the thing to remember—most of the time, alignment is not much of an issue in a DYI investment, unless you have partners . . ."

Paul grinned at his friend. "You know what I've learned over the last five years?"

Dan chuckled. "No—what?"

"If something is good, something bad is probably just around the corner!"

"I assume you're referring to your realization that investing yourself is bad for liquidity, but alignment isn't an issue . . . "

"That's exactly what I was thinking . . ."

Dan checked his watch. "We have an hour left before I have to take Linda over to the kids' . . . let's jump to the public market."

"Fine with me—I wrote down a couple of questions about alignment, but I can ask you later . . ."

"For most Canadians," Dan continued, "they use a public market to buy stocks, bonds, or a combination of both. You can buy stocks and-or bonds that are bundled together various ways—or, you can buy an ETF, or exchange-traded fund." Dan noticed Paul's eyebrows arch. "ETFs are fairly new, but provide a low-cost way to gain a diverse portfolio. In the public market, liquidity and alignment are much different than do-it-yourself investments—public markets are often terrific for liquidity. Many stocks and bonds trade in huge volumes five days a week and, unfortunately, some people throw a lot of that liquidity away. What a shame . . ."

"What goes wrong?"

"Inexperienced investors often buy something with front-end, or back-end fees—those commitments are usually there simply to pay commissions. If they did some research, they probably could have bought something—just as good—without any of the front-end or back-end fees . . ."

"There are fees for everything . . ."

"Yes, it seems like that—but, fees aren't always bad. If they pay the advisor for doing a great job, and result in your making money—terrific! But, fees that discourage you from cashing in your investment should be avoided . . ."

Paul looked as if the light went on. "So—that's how people throw away liquidity the public market provides?

Dan nodded. "That's one way—there's another way, too. Most people's public market investments are in their RRSPs. They may be able to sell the investments quickly, but if they try to access the cash for a personal reason, they end up having to pay some very significant taxes to get the money out. And, their right to buy those RRSPs is gone forever."

"Then, that's their fault for not thinking about it . . ."

"Well, yes—but did anyone warn them? When I prepare tax returns and I see RRSPs are being cashed in, I tell my clients they shouldn't buy RRSPs unless the funds can be left for the long term. To most, that was new information—I think they get talked into buying too much by the investment advisor—or, they get greedy by trying for too large of a tax refund."

Chapter Seventeen—The Market—Liquidity and Goals

"So, if I understand it, overall, the public markets get high marks on liquidity, but the investor can throw away this good feature by picking the wrong product, buying an RRSP, or both . . ."

Dan grinned. "Yep—that's about the size of it!"

Paul checked his watch. "How much time do we have?"

"About thirty minutes . . ."

"Okay—just kick me out when you need to . . ." He paused, looking at his notes. "How does the public market rate when it comes to alignment?

"Often, the alignment is lousy. Management of public companies are usually paid incredibly high salaries, and bonuses—even in years when the stock price drops. Sometimes, management is offered short-term incentives that actually drive them in ways hurting the long-term value of the stock." Dan shook his head. "I imagine lots of public companies are managed in ways that encourages long-term growth in the value of the stock—but, it seems everything I read is so negative."

"For instance . . ."

Dan scanned the bookshelves of the den. "I have a few books by Michael Lewis I can lend you—*The Big Short* was a super book about the big crash in 2008. *Boomerang* gets into some international finance issues, and *Flash Boys* is his latest . . ."

Paul focused on his friend—something seemed off. "You sound so negative—are you in the stock market yourself?"

Dan nodded. "Well—yes. And, I admit, I do love the liquidity—but, I never know when I might have to come up with a lot of cash in a hurry. Say you used up all of your cash to buy the building you operate from—maybe, shortly after, you can't bid on a big plumbing job because you didn't have the cash to finance the receivables. Turning down the contract would be painful . . ."

Paul nodded. "I get it—but, if I put the cash into the stock market, couldn't I be forced to liquidate at a poor time?"

"You're right—but timing is an issue with any investment. Surely that's better than not being able to get the cash, at all. And stocks and bonds are fairly easy to borrow against as long as they aren't in an RRSP . . ."

Paul glanced at his watch again. "I should get out of here—lend me those books, and Mandy and I will try to get ourselves up to speed . . ." Paul leapt up, waiting for his friend to do the same. "Before I go—I talked to a guy the other day, and he told me in 2007, with the encouragement of friends, he put a bunch of money in the stock market. In 2008, his stocks fell about 40%, and he panicked. He said his broker tried to talk him out of it, but he insisted everything should be sold. He will never invest in the stock market again . . ."

"Ah—those stories are all too common. This has been studied—people's actual results are far worse than the stock market indexes show . . ."

"Why?"

"Well, first of all, commissions. Yesterday, I was looking at how the TSX—the big Canadian exchange—moved over the last ten years. During the ten year period, the appreciation was about 4% per year, and commissions could easily take half of that. But, if you invested for eight or nine years, commissions will take virtually all the appreciation."

"That doesn't sound good!"

Dan laughed. "Luckily, getting dividends on your stocks

Chapter Seventeen—The Market—Liquidity and Goals

does improve things, but only by about 2%. Anyway, I suppose it's fair to say by investing for the long term, a return of about 4%, after paying commissions is realistic. Gaining a return of 4% vs. nothing is very important. Over ten years, your investment will rise by about 50%—which offsets inflation, so the money retains its value. However, most public market investors think they're going to do a lot better than that . . ."

"What about my friend who sold out in a panic?"

Dan shook his head. "Well—that's the other big reason people do badly. Our brains aren't naturally wired properly to make money in the stock market. Running with the herd is far too comfortable—like the guy you were talking to. Typically, the market has nice results for a while, so friends and family tell them how great being in the market is. But, after a long run of good results, a drop is almost inevitable."

"That seems obvious . . ."

"It's kind of cute the stock guys call such drops 'corrections' and, of course, inexperienced people tend to panic when that happens. Panic selling is terrible because, with patience, the stock market goes back up. The common saying is, 'Be nervous when others are happy, and happy when others are nervous.'" Dan grinned at Paul. "Easy to say, but so hard to do . . ."

"It sounds like poker—I play friendly games, but the old saying is 'get nervous if you look around and can't figure out who the sucker is.' Once in awhile, some young guy sits in, and bets more than he can handle. Once they get nervous they rarely win . . ."

Dan laughed, and got up. "Right you are—knowledge and experience are important in all aspects of life. Investing is no exception. You can gain knowledge by reading but, starting out, you have no experience. Generally, as a new investor, I would go slowly, investing in things low in risk. Avoid any kind of long-term commitment, or penalties for changing your mind."

"Did many of your clients make it big in the stock market?"

"Not many—most people who did well bought stocks with great long-term potential, then put them away for a long time. They only paid fees buying the stock, so no yearly fees. By ignoring the stocks, they didn't know about all the ups and downs—therefore, no panic selling." Dan headed toward the door of the den. "Now—I have to say this strategy may have flaws, but it worked. For the most part, I see the stock market as a place to get modest returns over the long run. You'll likely be wealthy, but it will probably be from plumbing or private investments—not the stock market."

The men headed for the front door. "Thanks for taking the time," Paul commented. "So—to sum up—for the public market, you believe the big advantage is liquidity, but you feel its record on management-investor alignment could be a lot better."

Dan nodded. "Correct . . ."

"But," Paul continued, "you think it's a reasonable place to get modest returns if you invest for the long run. Don't run with the pack by buying heavily when the prices are high, and no panic selling when prices drop. Educate yourself, keep fees to a minimum, and really understand what front-end or back-end fees are paying for . . ."

"That's it . . ."

"You mentioned a third type of investment or market called alternative . . ."

Dan held the door for his friend, "Yes, but we need to

leave that for another day. I know Linda is eager to see her grandkids, so I'll drop off the books I mentioned within the next couple of days..."

Paul grinned, shaking his neighbor's hand. "Go—get out of here! We'll talk later..."

Chapter Eighteen

Alternative Investments

As Paul knew would happen, taking Franklin for a walk became his responsibility. He didn't mind, though—Mandy had her hands full with the kids and, if he were to be completely honest, he grew fond of him over the years. The kids loved Franklin, and it turned out he was the perfect dog for their family.

The routine was twice a day, around the block three times and, on the Saturday before Halloween, Paul met up with Dan as he pulled up failing annual plants to prepare for winter.

"Paul! Franklin!" Dan brushed off the knees of his pants as he got up, extending his hand. "Out for a brisk walk?"

"We are . . ." Paul glanced at the sky. "If I didn't know better, I'd say we're in for a bit of snow soon . . ."

"My thought exactly," Dan agreed. "That's why I'm getting these out of the ground . . ."

Of course, Paul offered to help, but Dan declined. "What I want to know is," he said, "if you ever decided on your investments. What did you decide to do?"

"Strange you should ask—Mandy and I were talking about that just last night. The short answer is nothing . . ."

"What's the long answer?"

"Well, if you remember our last conversation, we were going to discuss alternative investments, but we didn't get around to it . . ."

"I remember—life gets in the way, doesn't it?"

Paul grinned. "I'm busy, that's for sure!"

Dan picked up the trowel, knocking off a few stubborn dirt clods. "So—alternative investments. What do you need to know?"

"Everything. Pros and cons . . ."

"Okay—well, they're good to discuss last because alternative investments are defined as something other than the classic investments such as publically traded stocks and bonds. That definition works well for big pension and university endowment funds."

"I figure big funds aren't keen on alternatives . . ."

"Maybe years ago—but today? Alternatives can easily exceed 50% of their portfolios. CPP invests in Saskatchewan farmland, and Harvard owns a massive amount of timberland in New Zealand."

Franklin looked up at Paul, then laid down on the sidewalk as if he figured theirs was going to be a long conversation.

Paul adjusted the leash. "For ordinary people, do alternatives include their houses and businesses they own and operate?"

Dan nodded. "Right—but in my own definition, I exclude those things because the average person thinks about their home and personally-run businesses differently."

"So what would be examples of alternative investing by guys like me?"

"Well, they might own private company's stocks or bonds, commodities such as gold, tax shelters, or hedge funds. Another example is some sort of co-ownership of real estate . . ."

"Where do they buy this stuff?"

"There are a few places—a stockbroker often has access, directly or indirectly."

"Indirectly?"

"Sure—for example, it might make sense to buy a company that owns gold mines instead of buying gold. Similarly, there are organizations you can invest in that have extensive holdings of residential apartments, or commercial buildings."

"Do you work for a stockbroker?"

Dan shook his head. "No—I work with an exempt market dealer, or EMD . . ."

"So—that's another place to buy alternative investments?"

"Yep . . ." He noticed Paul's confusion. "Let me explain—in Canada and before 2009, private, unregistered entities could approach potential investors, attempting to sell them debt or equity. I was an investor in a number of ventures and was treated well—but, many people had bad experiences. Often, governments—or, their securities exchanges—didn't know about problems until people were complaining."

"I saw things like that on T.V.—sad stories of naïve folks who lost all of their money on some flaky investment . . ."

Dan nodded. "That's right—the governments in Canada and their securities commissions felt greater regulations were needed. So, in 2009, new rules were brought in requiring people and organizations working in this industry to register with them—it was an effort to regulate them. The exchanges can—and, do—check compliance with the rules, even when no one complained. The newly regulated industry is termed the 'exempt market', and securities sold this way are called 'exempt or private securities.'"

"Why are they exempt?"

"To sell investments in Canada, the investment must have a 'prospectus' . . ."

"What's that?"

Dan laughed. "There are a bunch of words to learn, aren't there? A prospectus is a large, legally-worded description of the investment reviewed by the securities commission. The word exempt means there is some sort of exemption from a prospectus available, thereby allowing the EMD to sell a specific person a specific security."

Paul leveled a look at his friend. "You see this face? Do I look confused?"

Dan erupted with one of his belly laughs. "Well, the truth is the rules are still evolving, but, typically you need to be fairly wealthy or have a high yearly income. Sometimes, less wealthy people can invest depending on whether the investment is small, or whether certain documents were issued. It can also depend on what province you live in—some investments can be put in registered plans like RRSPs. Assuming you can invest, the investment dealer will need to keep notes on your financial situation to ensure why the investment was suitable for you . . ."

Paul leaned down to give Franklin a few pats on his head. Over the years, he evolved from an incorrigible dog to a well-trained pooch and, no matter how long Paul stopped to chat with someone along the way, Franklin remained patient and contented to take a load off in the middle of the sidewalk. "So, I would sit down with someone like you," Paul asked, "to find out what's available, and whether I would qualify to buy the investments?"

"Yes—but the information I gathered would have to be reviewed by the compliance people at the EMD. They have the final say on whether the deal can proceed. It's a big responsibility for me and the dealership . . ."

"Where do these securities come from?"

"There are organizations offering them, and they're called 'issuers'. Ideally, the issuers should be completely independent—they meet with one or more EMD, and the EMD decides what they will and will not sell. If the EMD decides to sell the securities, they then give the information to their investment dealers, like me. Finally, I decide if the security is appropriate for my clients." Dan paused for a moment. "I should point out the issuer and the EMD are not always independent—that doesn't have to be the case but, in my opinion, independence is best for the investor."

"Why is that?"

"Well, creating a new product can be difficult and costly. If an EMD goes through the creation process, odds are there will be a lot of pressure on the company's sales force to sell it, regardless of how good it is . . ."

"Yes, but isn't that pretty common in all industries?"

"True—but the exceptions are nice. Think about Charlie who owns our local sporting goods store—he obviously cares about his long-term reputation. If Charlie sold you poor hockey pads, you aren't likely to be a return customer. So, guys like Charlie try to pick goods his customer will appreciate . . ."

"Let me see if I understand you correctly—you're saying it's better if an EMD isn't selling their own internally produced products . . ."

"Yes . . ."

"Should that apply to all investments? Even public ones?"

"Again, yes—I think so. I encourage you to ask questions about independence and conflicts with any financial advisor, and financial institution with which you work . . ."

Paul paused, watching Franklin lick something on the sidewalk. "But—how does an EMD decide what to sell?"

"It should be a strict, due-diligence process, ideally led by properly qualified people. Probably the best educational designation is a Chartered Financial Analyst, or CFA. The EMD should focus on managements' industry experience as well as the track record. Obviously, the EMD also has to like the business fundamentals." Dan, too, watched Franklin for a moment. "Remember alignment? The EMD should be looking for strong alignment between the goals of the issuer's management and the investors . . ."

"What about liquidity?"

Chapter Eighteen—Alternative Investments

"Good question—the exempt security might be more liquid than a do-it-yourself investment, but far less liquid than the public market. My approach is to make sure your needs for liquidity are met by other sources."

Paul nodded. "That makes sense—what about risk?"

"Of course, I need to look at whether you can generally cope with risk. Less liquidity is only one risk, but there are many risks in investments, and no two investments are exactly alike. It's important you work with someone who will help you learn about and understand the risks. And, that your individual investment isn't too large. Maybe that's the most important lesson—not all your eggs in one basket. We need to look at all of your investments, and consider whether you are well diversified . . ."

"What if I only like real estate?"

"In that case and at the very least, we should try to put you into different types of real estate in different geographic areas. Farmland in Saskatchewan, and commercial land near Dallas are pretty different."

"What if I change my mind after a year or so?"

"That would be a challenge because, typically, there is limited ability to cash the investments in early. Say the issuer's plan is to buy raw land, rezone it, and sell it in about five years. The issuer isn't going to have extra cash lying around to help investors who want out early. Yes, you might be able to sell your investment to someone, but how would you know what a fair value is? Frankly, selling at a discount can be tough—you have to look at the issuer's plan before you buy. And, just because the expected time frame is five years, the investment could actually turn into cash in two years—or, ten years."

Paul noticed his porch light flicker on—it would be dark within minutes. "But what if I had almost all of my money in an investment that was badly delayed?"

"It shouldn't happen because your purchase shouldn't exceed 5% of your net worth. If I tried to put you into something a lot bigger, the EMD should be rejecting the deal."

"So—is this an advantage over do-it-yourself investments?"

"Exactly. A big problem with do-it-yourself is having way too much of your net worth in a single deal. Or, you might be an expert in an unrelated industry to what you are investing in. But, on the other hand, if you owned ten investments—public or exempt—the odds of some sort of hiccup is higher simply because you own ten things. Hopefully, the problem is just a hiccup, and not a gulp . . ."

Paul cued Franklin it was time to go by gently tugging on his leash. "Knowing what you know," he asked, "what would you suggest for someone like me?"

"Although it's risky, you will probably only get wealthy from do-it-yourself investments like your plumbing business. But, as time goes on, the business will have a lot more cash than it needs. So, to lower your risk, it would be great to diversify—ensure liquidity needs are met by having enough cash, or public market investments. Personally, I look for a broker who understands the need to include alternative investments and foreign stocks along with traditional Canadian investments. Look at their track record—how did their advice pan out in times of crisis like 2008? Once your needs for liquidity are taken care of, I suggest looking at exempt investments due to higher expected rates of return. However, the selection of the EMD as well as the salesperson from that EMD are critically important—if you can't find

Chapter Eighteen—Alternative Investments

people you can trust, keep looking. I wouldn't listen to any salesperson I don't trust."

"How will I know I can trust them?"

"Simple—their track record . . ."

Chapter Nineteen

Retirement—Paul Wants a Plan

As you probably noticed, Paul and Mandy love to plan—and, they're good at it. Would the young plumber's business have been so successful if he didn't plan for its opening far in advance? Maybe. But, chances are good the answer is no—and, without Dan's advice over the years? Well—that was invaluable. Having Dan in his corner made all the difference, so it made sense Paul would pick his brain about the ins and outs of retirement. But, by the time he could make time for a learning session it was Halloween, and the kids were looking forward to dressing up to scare the neighbors, as well as a fabulous amount of goodies in their bags.

Naturally, their first stop was Dan and Linda's. Linda answered the door with Dan in tow, both throwing up their hands in mock fright as they reacted to Harry's and Maggie's costumes—a witch and Batman always works.

They chatted for a few minutes before moving on to the next house, the two men agreeing to get together the following day for sports and a beer. The truth was Paul looked forward to hanging out with his friend—between work, Mandy, and the kids there was little time for himself, and it would be nice to relax with his friend, catching up on time passed.

****

"So," Dan asked as they settled into the den easy chairs, "did Harry and Maggie cash in last night?"

Paul laughed as he thought about bags of candy being dumped out on their kitchen table the night before. "You can only have one a day," Mandy warned. But, she knew she would cave and let them have two. "Cashing in doesn't even describe it! As soon as we got home Mandy took control, much to their dismay!"

"Trust me—those are some of the best memories you'll ever have . . ."

Paul nodded, and was quiet for a moment. "Time doesn't stop, that's for sure—which is why I'm already thinking about retirement. I have been for quite some time . . ."

"You're smart . . ."

Chapter Nineteen—Retirement—Paul Wants a Plan

"I know Mandy and I need a plan, but it seems to me any plan over ten years is kind of silly. I'm closing on thirty-five and, overall, everything's great—what I can't figure out is where I'll be in ten years." Paul paused as Dan cracked open his beer. "I want the option of partial retirement by the time I hit fifty-five, if possible—the business is making about $400,000 a year, and I paid off Nick as well as my line of credit. I'm thinking profits will increase slightly over time, but the business is about as large as I can comfortably manage..."

"You're wise to realize where you're most comfortable."

"Mandy and I only spend around $100,000 per year, so we expect the cash will pile up quickly..."

"Did you ever meet with the two investment guys I referred—one for public markets and the other for the exempt market?"

"I did—overall, I think they can get us a return of around 7% a year—the investment income will be about 55% interest income. The other 45% should be split roughly equally between capital gains and dividends. Other than that? I don't have a clue..." Paul looked at his friend, grinning. "You know that's why I'm here..."

Dan returned the grin. "I do, indeed! So, let's start with assumptions—which assumption are you unsure of?"

"Well—I know the plumbing business pretty well, and Mandy and I are careful with spending. Frugal, actually. So, for me, the rate of return on investments seems like a wild guess..."

"I agree..." Dan thought for a moment, thinking of how he could best explain it. "Let's look at two things—rates of 7% and 4%—so we can see what the difference is..."

Paul wasn't sure, but that sounded like a lot of work. "Sounds great—but, isn't that a lot for you to do?"

"Not really—just a few hours. Now, if I did the calculations precisely, that would take some time. But, I can also use averages and get pretty accurate results—that's a lot faster. I know from experience the rate of return earned on investments has a huge impact, and we're guessing between 4% and 7%. Therefore, there's no point in getting terribly precise with calculations in other areas . . ."

"Okay—but, let me do something for you. Remember I recommended you put in a lot more shut-off valves? They sure come in handy if anything pops—you know in the time it takes to turn off the main basement shut-off, a lot of damage can happen. And—if you want to replace anything—you don't have to turn off all the water while you work on one area . . ."

"That's really not necessary, Paul . . ."

"It is for me—so, please let me do this for you as thanks for doing this plan for us . . ."

Dan eyed his friend. "Deal . . ."

****

Paul emerged from underneath the kitchen cabinets, wiping his hands on a paper towel. "That's it for this trip—three shut-off valves installed. I think another three will do

Chapter Nineteen—Retirement—Paul Wants a Plan

the trick..."

"Excellent! And, I also have your plan done—do you have time to go over it now? Then you can explain it to Mandy..."

"Yep—good timing, too. Mandy took the kids to the mall..."

Paul brushed off the back of his pants before plopping into Dan's soft, den chair. "So—what does the plan look like?"

"Well—at first, it's pretty simple—with a business income of $400,000 and personal spending of $100,000, your total taxes will be about $66,000. That leaves $234,000 going into company investments." Dan glanced at Paul. "It's important your company owns the investments rather than you, personally."

"Why?"

"Because holding the investments personally increases the taxes by $63,000—you wind up saving a lot less. Because of personal taxes on dividends, you would have to pay to give you the cash in your personal name to buy them. That's a drop of 27%. Of course, we can't ignore the fact those taxes will be paid one day, but it's a very long tax deferral. Odds are the tax won't be paid until you and Mandy pass away—that could easily be fifty years from now..."

"So, if the company saves $234,000 a year, shouldn't we end up with about 2.3 million after ten years?"

Dan nodded. "Probably more—but how much more depends heavily on the rate of return your investment advisors get you—that's the net of commissions and income taxes. At 4%, the 2.3 million grows to 2.9. At 7%, it's 3.5 million. It's interesting how key that rate of return is to your retirement—if you were to retire in ten years and the investment income was 4% all along, the monthly income before tax is roughly $10,000. But—at 7%, the investment income more than doubles."

"Do we need to keep living on a $100,000 a year for the whole ten years?"

Nope—I had to increase your dividends to avoid company refundable taxes. Toward the end of the ten years—using the 7% rate—you could be taking out about $12,000 a month. If you didn't take it out, the company would owe you the money, tax free, since your personal dividend income would be larger than your draws."

"Do the income taxes shoot up over time?"

"Not really—at first, it's about $66,000 a year. But, on average, with adding the investment income, tax only goes up to $89,000 a year . . ."

Paul's eyebrows shot up. "Surely, the increase should be more than $23,000—you said the income was over $20,000 a month . . ."

"True—but remember I'm using averages when I do the projection. The average investment income is something like $180,000 a year. We assumed the breakdown was $100,000 interest, $40,000 of eligible dividend income and $40,000 of capital gains. For a company, there is no permanent tax on the dividends—only refundable taxes that we're avoiding by paying dividends to you and Mandy." Dan paused to glance at the score, and grab a second beer.

"Capital gains," he continued, "are only half taxable. So the investment income averages out to $120,000—$100,000 of interest and $20,000 of taxable capital gains. The corporate tax rate on investment income is only 20%—this is $21,600. Also remember our total taxes were, on average, $23,000—the difference is a bit of extra personal tax, and it increases because we have to pay out dividends to avoid the company paying refundable taxes. But—there's also good news—before investment income, we only paid you ineligible dividends. Now, we can make some of those dividends eligible—or, tax free—because the company's investment income includes eligible dividends *and* capital gains. Overall, your personal taxes go up a bit, but not very much considering you have the ability to spend $35,000 a year more. It's actually a super deal..."

Paul grinned. "It sounds pretty complicated to me!"

"You're right—it is. You'll need help from your public accountant, especially with the eligible and capital dividends. And, accounting for investment income isn't easy either. Frankly, I expect you'll see your accounting fees double over time—these are tricky issues, and the accountant needs to do a great job, year by year..."

"I figured. Are there restrictions when it comes to my company investments?"

"Nope. None. Registered plans like RRSPs and TFSAs however, do have restrictions—but there aren't similar rules for companies. You can buy raw land, commercial real estate, and anything else you can think of..."

"What about a summer cottage?"

"You could, but it's not a good idea. For a personal-use property such as a cottage, it's best held in your personal name. Otherwise, you should be paying a market rent to your company when you use it..."

"I really don't have time for a summer cottage—I was just wondering..."

Dan leveled a look at his friend. "Right..."

"Obviously, this plan is critically important to me—how can we track how we're doing?"

"Funny you should mention that—I made up a schedule for you to follow. Just add up the value of your investments one year from now, and each year after that. Compare the actual value to what the schedule says..."

"Thanks! So—what do I need to concentrate on to make this plan work?"

"First—keep your business income up there. Second—don't spend beyond the plan's limits. Third—make sure the funds are being invested on a timely basis. Finally—track your actual rates of return. Remember what a dramatic effect that had? Unfortunately, too many business couples ignore it because they say they're too busy. I understand, but it's a shame—it's not a long list of tasks, but it's still a challenge."

Paul nodded. "I get that—however, there are areas in which I can do better than we assumed. The easiest one—for me—is to make more in my business..."

"I agree—but keep in mind your business might need some of the extra cash for replacing equipment, or financing increased receivables."

As Paul thought about the future, he found it incredible, at age forty-five, he and Mandy could have over 3 million in investments, and he told Dan so. "Who retires at age forty-five?" he commented. To him, it seemed a little weird.

"Well, don't worry about it. You probably won't retire even if the investments hit 3 million. Your kids will still be young and, most likely, you'll decide to work less." Dan paused, allowing time for his words to sink in. "And, of course," he finally advised, "many things can go wrong..."

"That I know—Mandy and I always prepare for the

Chapter Nineteen—Retirement—Paul Wants a Plan

unexpected . . ."

"One thing . . ." Dan added. "As my clients got older, I noticed I had a lot more wealthy plumbers than doctors. What I should really say is my owners of good companies were wealthier than most of my professional clients . . ."

"How so?"

"The doctors spent so much time getting educated, their incomes were delayed, and they often had huge student loans. They also tend to buy bigger houses as well as newer, fancier cars. It wasn't always true, but the doctors often spent a lot more on daily expenses—that's okay, I guess, but every single one of those issues delays a comfortable retirement."

"Then why didn't they get financial planning advice?"

"Who knows? Maybe they thought they didn't need it. But I notice now more professionals are getting help with financial planning—hopefully, their prospects for retirement will improve . . ."

"Well, at least we're not going to be in that boat! What other issues should Mandy and I consider?"

Dan thought for a moment before answering. "Well—you should think about estate planning. It isn't all about the size of the investment portfolio—so, some day, we should discuss using a holding company or a family trust. There are a couple of simpler things—such as TFSAs and RESPs—that come to mind. Not big issues, mind you, but still worth talking about. What's weird is these plans aren't as good for business owners like you and Mandy, and they aren't discussed often . . ."

Paul checked his watch. "Gotta go! Another time?"

Dan grinned. "Of course! Get out of here!"

Chapter Twenty

RESPs and TFSAs—Do They Fit?

With Paul's extensive knowledge about financial planning as well as estate planning and retirement—thanks to Dan—he knew there were only a few more things he needed to consider. Even though Paul completely understood the importance of such planning, he still thought it was a little weird he was thinking about twenty or thirty years down the road. "A bit of a time warp," he commented as he resumed his conversation with his neighbor.

"Indeed—and, because of that very feeling, many young people don't want to talk about their future . . ."

"I get it—but, if I hadn't followed your advice, I don't think our business would be so successful . . ."

"You know I'm glad to help—so, what's the topic for

today?"

"RESPs and TFSAs—my bank has all kinds of handouts, but we never discussed them. What do you think?"

Dan thought for a moment. "Well—there's a common factor that makes them less attractive for most business owners—so, I suppose, that's why we haven't talked about it. The bottom line is you need to take money out of your company before you can buy into either of those personal programs—corporations can't participate. Since nothing is owing to you, it means you need to declare an ineligible dividend—and, in the third tax bracket, you'll pay about 26% tax. We talked before about eligible and ineligible dividends, but even with an eligible dividend, your tax is still 15%—most people don't save using a company. So for them, directing savings to one of those funds costs them nothing." Dan paused, thinking about what Paul needed to know. "I think we should discuss both plans just for general information. But—before you get too excited—remember the big up front cost that's an issue for most business owners . . ."

Paul grinned. "I have a feeling I need to be writing this down . . ."

Dan let out one of his famous belly laughs, then handed Paul a legal pad and pen. "Good idea . . ." He settled into his chair, making a tent with his fingers. "Let's start with TFSAs—Tax Free Savings Accounts . . ."

"I sure do love the sound of any tax free government program!"

Dan smiled. "I bet you do! So—you probably know the basics, but let's go over them to be on the safe side." He paused as Paul scribbled on the legal pad. "The program started in 2009, and the original idea was you can save $5,000 per year, and income you earn isn't taxed. In 2013, the $5,000 was

Chapter Twenty—RESPs and TFSAs—Do They Fit?

increased to $5,500—that means by 2015, the accumulated amount is $36,500..."

"That's pretty good, don't you think? It sounds like a lot of tax savings..."

"At first blush, yes—but do the math. Say you buy a 1% GIC, and you're in a 32% bracket—how much tax are you actually saving?"

Paul took a moment to calculate. "Well—the income would be $365 per year, so I suppose the tax savings are only around $120 a year..."

"That's about right—and, some places charge a fee. For example's sake, say that's $100 per year. Aren't you only up $20? That's a tiny amount for the hassle involved. As it pertains to you, to net $36,500—personally—you would be cashing in almost $49,000 in company investments, paying tax on the dividend of around $12,000 to have the funds to put into the TFSA..."

Paul clicked his pen several times, thinking. "So—as I understand it—a 1% GIC seems like a waste of time. But, what if I want to invest in raw land or rental properties?"

"The limit of $36,500 is too small—plus, you can only invest in the kinds of things an RRSP can own..."

"What if I bought a high risk stock? It could double in value, or fall to nothing—how would that work?"

"It works out well if it doubles. Let's say it doubles to $73,000, and you sell it—now, your TFSA limit is $73,000. If you invest it, you'll enjoy a return of 5% a year—the income is $3,650 a year, and you pay no tax on the income..."

Paul smiled. "What if I cashed it in, and bought a hot car? Any tax then?"

"Nope—it's not like an RRSP. The TFSA is saving money on which the tax is already paid."

Again, Paul clicked his pen. "Okay—so, if I bought the hot car in January and inherited money in June, can I put $73,000 back into my TFSA account?"

"Negative—but you can as long as you wait until the following January. Otherwise, you'll get a nasty letter from CRA and very likely you will be paying a penalty. Sadly, around 100,000 Canadians make that mistake every year..."

"What happens if my risky investment fails, and the stock is of no value? Obviously, my plan is earning nothing—can I sell the stock and collapse my plan to get my limit back?"

Dan grinned. "Nope, again—all you can do is wait for the next January, and your plan limit goes up by $5,500 like everyone else's. But, your limit in January 2016 is only $5,500. People who hadn't used a TFSA would have a limit in 2016 of $42,000..."

"It seems to me—in my situation—I'm better off investing inside my company."

"That's right—you don't pay the tax by taking out the dividend. Remember how we talked about what a good deal capital gains are in a company? The company only pays 10% on the total capital gain, and personal savings from having a capital gain will likely exceed that. We're naturally wired to try to avoid triggering income and the related tax, but it's always best to push the numbers before making decisions."

"There goes buying a hot car with tax-free money!" Paul laughed at the thought of having such a dream car.

"I do think," Dan continued, "TFSAs can work for business owners in some cases—such as when you have a

Chapter Twenty—RESPs and TFSAs—Do They Fit?

big shareholders' loan, and can withdraw the funds you need without paying tax. From there, I would consider the type of income the qualified investment will generate—if the income is significant and either interest or business income, the TFSA can work well. But, the saving is unlikely to ever be significant—let's say you built your TFSA up all the way to $100,000 and you earn a 10% return in the form of interest or business income. In a 40% tax bracket, we're still only talking about saving tax of $4,000 per year. Sure, it's nice, but hardly a game changer . . ."

Paul nodded. "Agreed—so let's move on to RESPs . . ."

"Well, as you know, RESP stands for Registered Education Savings Plans, and they've been around longer. Of course, the basic idea is to help parents save for their kids' higher education—but let's jump to why you might be interested . . ."

"Isn't there some sort of grant?"

"Yep—you put in $2,500 a year per child to a maximum of $36,000. The government then contributes 20%—so, for you, that's a maximum of $7,200. If the plan has income over the years of $6,800, then the total plan is worth $50,000. Plus, there's additional help for low-income families, and a few provinces contribute—but, only Quebec's is significant."

"Is the whole thing tax free to take out?"

Dan shook his head. "No—but think about it. It makes sense the $36,000 is tax free because that was tax-paid money. But, both the grant and income are taxable, typically to the student—normally, they have a bunch of tuition and low income while a student, so it may seem tax free. The truth is, however, there's long-run tax cost of about 25% since the income normally chews up future tax savings . . ."

Paul didn't quite understand. "Why?"

"Because students often have unused tuition tax credits when they graduate. If the RESP reduces those tuition credits, then the government gets their pound of flesh—eventually."

"Then—what's so great about an RESP?"

"Just this—the grant of $7,200 is found money, but, if you lose roughly 25% to tax, one way or the other the net amount the family is ahead is $5,400 per child. If you have four kids—well, you do the math . . ."

"That's over $20,000—but it seems to me a good way to lose control of the kids. Wouldn't I be putting a lot of money into their names?"

"Yes, and no. Personally I prefer family plans . . ."

"Is that the same as a group plan?"

Again, Dan shook his head. "No—I wouldn't do a group plan. Group plans are where you pool in with other contributors, and the plans tend to have higher fees and more restrictive rules. The way I like to do it is to wait until I know the family will be at least two kids—as the contributor, you get to decide which kid gets what. The child will get the cheque made out in his or her name, but, in my family, I had the child turn the funds back to me. Often, I cashed out the RESP as quickly as possible." Dan hesitated for a minute, thinking about the process. "But," he continued, "it's a hassle. Normally the student has to get a letter from the educational institution saying they are enrolled, and there are limits in terms of how fast the money can be taken out . . ."

"I don't want to be too personal, but did you give the kids the money?"

Dan nodded. "I think it is a parent's decision—in our

Chapter Twenty—RESPs and TFSAs—Do They Fit?

case, we funded the tuition up to their first degree, and we let them live at home without paying room or board. So, we paid out more than what was in the RESP—but, the point is we told the kids what we were paying or not paying had nothing to do with the government plan."

Paul crossed out a few words on his pad. "What about the issue of taking out the funds from the company?"

"Good question—if paying kids' tuition is something you will do eventually, then the funds need to come out at one point or another. The downside I see is, perhaps, you have killer investments in your company that you just can't do in a RESP plan. Again, do the math. The grant is only worth roughly $5,000 per child—maybe that's not enough to offset moving to much poorer investments."

"What if none of the kids go to university?"

"Then you will end up with a bit of a mess on your hands. Essentially, you can get the original contributions back, but the government grants will be going back to the government. The income you earned can be transferred to a RRSP, so it ends up being eventually taxed."

Paul chewed on what he learned during their conversation. "So—overall—you aren't a big fan of TFSAs for most business owners, and you advise to do the math before making a decision. For RESPs, you like the grants, but you would tell people to do some research on the rules." He paused a moment. "It sounds as if the only plan you like is a family plan—and, you make sure the kids know what you are prepared to do for them has nothing to do with the size of the RESP . . ."

Dan nodded. "Good job!"

"Cool—but I have one final question. A lot of kids are

not going to university these days—do those kids just lose out?"

Dan nodded. "I think it's a decision you need to face. Linda and I thought it was only fair to do something to help out kids who don't go to post-secondary school . . ."

Chapter Twenty-one

Holding Companies

"There's nothing quite like a spring thaw in January, is there?" Dan stopped for a few moments as Paul's dog explored a new scent.

"Agreed—it's nice to take Franklin on a long walk again!"

Dan reached down to give Franklin a few pats on his head, scratching a few time behind the ears. "It's been an interesting winter, that's for sure . . ."

Paul tugged on the leash. "So—I was chatting with a couple of guys on my beer league hockey team, and they were talking about having a holding company like it was the best thing since sliced bread . . ."

"True—but so are high blood pressure pills if you have high blood pressure."

Paul looked at him, perplexed. "So, perhaps a solution to a problem—but make sure there is a problem?"

"You got it . . ."

Paul watched as Franklin took stock of a mailbox post. "So—what problem do they solve?"

"Well—there are a couple. First, say you and Mandy owned half the plumbing company, and the other owners—also a couple—disagreed on how to invest excess cash. Maybe they'll only buy GIC's—but, you and Mandy are happier with investments showing higher returns and risk. To invest personally, you would need to pay big dividends, and that could trigger something like 25% to 30% personal tax."

"Ah—I see the problem. I take it both couples should have a holding company—how does that work?"

"Each couple could own their own holding company, and it would own your 50% interest in the plumbing company. A dividend from the plumbing company to the holding company should be tax free. Of course, you'll still pay personal tax if you move the funds out of the holding company into your personal names, but that could be many years later."

Paul stopped, and so did Franklin. "So—if we started the business with another couple, should we have had holding companies right from the beginning . . ."

"Not necessarily—extra companies do create extra administrative cost. It could be many years before there was substantial cash lying around."

"But do we trigger tax if we set it up later?"

"You shouldn't be taxable—the government allows you to fix that using a special election. But, you'll need professional help, and that won't be cheap—it could be as much as $5,000 per couple. Typically, however, at that point

Chapter Twenty-one—Holding Companies

there's a lot of cash on hand to pay for it."

Paul thought for a minute. "But it won't apply to Mandy and me since we own the entire plumbing company—is that right?"

"True—there is, however, a second problem holding companies can partially address . . ."

"I'm listening!"

"The problem is creditor protection. What if your company gets sued for more than it's worth? The creditor may not be able to sue you personally since you are a shareholder—but losing everything the company owns would be pretty awful. Let's say down the road the company had operating assets like equipment and receivables of 1 million, but it also owned 2 million in investments. Do you see you would be better off with having a holding company owning the investments?"

"Maybe . . ."

"Explain . . ."

"What if the investment were an apartment building, and I were sued because someone slipped on the sidewalk? Since the holding company owns the apartment and the plumbing company, wouldn't I still lose everything?"

Dan nodded. "Yes, that's true. But, I need to make an important point—insurance was created for a good reason. Of course, you want to insure all the risks you can identify, and you'll need the help of your general insurance agent. If you're convinced you have no uninsured reasonably identifiable risks, then maybe you don't need a holding company . . ."

By this time, Franklin decided it was time to take a load

off, plopping down right in front of Paul's feet. "Right. One of the guys on my hockey team said he had a holding company because his construction company employees could get hurt on the job. But that doesn't make sense to me..."

Dan thought for a second, trying to figure out what Paul was talking about. "Ah—he must have Workers' Compensation coverage that would deal with a claim like that."

"I think that's the case—but, I get your point. I should work with my insurance agent and lawyer to see if they recognize uninsurable risks such as a massive job going sideways..."

Dan gave Paul a knowing look. "Remember, though, I said a holding company can only partially address this issue."

"Why?"

"Because the operating company must declare dividends to the holding company before the problem occurs—and often small business owners only declare dividends once a year."

"Does that mean operating assets are always at risk?"

Dan shook his head. "Not necessarily—you might be able to declare dividends to eliminate retained earnings in the operating company. Then, the holding company could lend the money back—much like taking back security the way your bank would."

"Might?"

"I say might because your bank and bonding company may have committed you to a certain level of net assets (or retained earnings)—you can't violate those commitments. And, if you need more support from those people down the road, they aren't going to be too happy seeing those creditor protection steps you took. After all, these people are important creditors—even suppliers may wish to see your balance sheet before they give you credit. So, sucking out all the retained earnings and making your holding company a preferred creditor isn't going to please them—to put it mildly."

"So—I guess there's a balance somewhere. No doubt, I need to talk to my insurance agent and lawyer about this stuff. I need to insure the risks I can—knowing my uninsurable risks—and keep the operating company strong enough for creditors, including the bank and bonding company. But, if I can move significant assets to a holding company, look into it..."

"Right—but keep your accountant in the loop, too. For example, say you had an apartment building in the plumbing company that's worth a lot more than its value for tax purposes. It might have gone up in value, but you may also have depreciated it so its present tax value is even less than you paid for it. Changing the ownership to your holding company triggers a sale—at fair market value—for tax purposes. Your accountant and lawyer may be able to assist you, but it's very tricky stuff."

Paul tugged on Franklin's leash, signaling it was time to go. "So—before I start buying big investments like this, I should consider getting a holding company..."

"That's right—but the overall point is to talk to all the professionals you rely upon..."

Paul grinned, shaking hands with his friend. "Thanks, Dan—backyard barbecue soon? I just got a new smoker I'm itching to try..."

Chapter Twenty-two

The estate plan

Mandy looked at her husband fondly. "I can't believe you're going to be forty-five next week—and I'm already forty-four!"

Paul busted out a belly laugh! "Well—the kids are teenagers—how does that make you feel?"

He looked at his wife, loving her more at that moment than he ever had. Their operating company was making about 1 million a year, and their holding company had 5 million in investments—rental properties, public stocks, and exempt investments. The holding company owned the operating company, so Paul and Mandy figured it was a good time to understand the ins and outs of estate planning. Who will they go to for the best advice?

Yep. Dan . . .

Only this time it was different—Paul and Mandy

outgrew their home next to Dan and Linda, and they rarely got to see their good friend. So, have a confab about estate planning would bring back fond memories of their time as neighbors.

Paul shook his ex-neighbor's hand with enthusiasm. "It's great to see you! We sure miss having you next door, but, you'll be glad to know the last few years have treated us well! It looks as if they've been kind to you, as well!"

Dan laughed. "I can see that! Come in! Come in!"

The good friends made themselves comfortable, just like old times. After they settled in their respective chairs, Paul took a long look at Dan—time treated him well. "We feel we could retire," he began, "but we're just too young. Besides, with the kids still in public school, we need to be around."

"A good thought . . ." He called to Mandy from across the room where she and Linda were looking at pictures of the kids. "What does life look like for you these days, Mandy?"

"Fun, but busy. I watch over the company's bookkeeper and put the monthly financials together—the holding company investments are time-consuming." Mandy grinned at Dan. "You know we have to be a taxi since the kids aren't quite old enough to drive . . ."

"Ah, yes—I remember those days well, And, I wouldn't give them up for anything!"

Paul nodded. "Time's too short—Mandy and I lost a couple of friends lately, and it really has us thinking about estate planning. Interestingly, your name came up . . ." He grinned, and winked at Mandy.

"Just like old times, eh? Well—I used to do this a lot, but please make sure you talk to your lawyer and accountant. The laws in this area are provincial, so also be careful about

Chapter Twenty-two—The Estate Plan

what you read."

"Examples?"

"Well—many provinces have high probate fees, but Alberta does not. So, articles written in Ontario focusing on keeping probate fees down have little application in Alberta."

Mandy piped up. "I've heard of probate, but I have no idea of what it is . . ."

"Good question. Few people understand why probate is needed—but, let's go over the basics first . . ."

"Is it complicated," Paul asked.

"Not really—first, both of you should have three documents in place. If you knew with certainty you would die suddenly, then you would only need a will. But, most of us have a long period of disability which brings up two issues. Someone needs to handle your money—even paying your bills."

"We haven't thought about that . . ."

"The solution is a leaping and enduring power of attorney. A general power of attorney gives someone the ability to sign on your behalf—leaping means it leaps into action if you are mentally incapable. Most powers of attorney stop being effective if you become mentally disabled, but if you make them enduring, they continue to be effective in spite of your problem."

"That sounds like a good thing—what's the second issue?"

"It's what Americans call a living will. Basically, you want your opinion known on decisions like when to pull the plug. In Canada, it's more likely called a personal directive.

Typically, lawyers have good standard wording that fits what most people want."

Paul thought for a moment, glancing at Mandy. "I think we both have all three documents, so I suppose we're covered."

"Maybe—most people don't realize their will only deals with the assets that are left for the executor to administer."

Mandy picked up on that one. "Isn't that everything?"

"Not always. Have you ever named someone in a document as your beneficiary? It's pretty common with life insurance and RRSPs . . ."

Paul fielded the answer. "Sure—that would be Mandy in both cases."

"Right—so those are examples where the asset's ownership changes the moment you die, and your will has no say. This is also the case if you own something in joint tenancy—the last joint tenant gets it all. A really common example is your house—couples often own their house this way . . ."

"So the executor only deals with assets that are left?"

"Yep—if, initially, you and Mandy want to leave everything to each other, you could have every asset dealt with either by joint tenancy, or by making each other beneficiaries. If there's nothing to do, you really don't need an executor and you don't pay probate fees either. However, you should still have a will because you might miss something—not to mention you need to deal with the possibility you both may die at the same time."

Paul thought for a moment. "Let's talk about probate—what's the purpose of it?"

Chapter Twenty-two—The Estate Plan

"Well—it's sort of a solution to a problem. Let's say a widower died, and he only has one asset—a big savings account in the Royal Bank. He leaves it—in his will—to his only son. Then, the Royal Bank hands over the money after seeing the will. Six months later, Dad's church shows up with a will dated the day before he died, leaving everything to the church. So, the church sues the Royal Bank—because of this possibility, you can understand the bank not wanting to turn over the cash even though there seems to be a valid will . . ."

"But that could drag things out for years!"

"Indeed! So, the provincial governments provide a solution—if you take the right steps, they grant you probate. You can take the probate to the bank, and they'll hand over the funds to the executor . . ."

"But how does that guarantee there isn't a second will?"

"It doesn't—but, in my example, the province would pay the church. This doesn't happen very often . . ."

Paul thought about that for a minute or two. "I can see people wanting to use this system with kids, as well. Put everything in joint name, or name them as beneficiaries. Your will becomes irrelevant when it's time for the kids to inherit. No need for an executor or probate—right?"

"Correct. Some people try using these tools, but it's often a bad idea especially when there's more than one child."

"What do you mean?"

"For example—I had a client whose wife passed away. He had two sons, and two assets—his RRSP was worth about 1 million, and he figured the tax on the RRSP would be about $400,000. He left the RRSP to his oldest son by naming him as a beneficiary."

"What about his house? Did he have one?"

Dan nodded. "He did, and it was worth around $600,000. He could have put the son down as a joint tenant, but what he did was change his will making his youngest son the only beneficiary."

"Okay—you lost me. So, don't both get about $600,000?"

"No—the problem is the estate has to pay the tax on the RRSP. The oldest son gets the entire RRSP of 1 million, and the youngest pays the $400,000 tax bill from selling the house—so he only gets $200,000."

"That hardly seems equitable..."

"True, the oldest son can fix the problem by just paying his brother $400,000, and all is well—however, he doesn't have to."

"Our wills simply say we first leave everything to each other, and then it all goes 50-50 to our kids when they turn 21. Is that common?"

"Very. And, a simple will like this avoids another pitfall —specifically giving assets to people..."

"How so?"

"The first thing is you don't want to be changing your will all the time. Say you left your TD Bank GIC's to your son, and a rental property to your daughter because they were of similar value. But, before you die, you cash in or sell one of these assets, and don't change your will. One child inherits way more than the other—something that could drive your kids apart after you die."

Paul nodded, and glanced at Mandy. "Well, I think we're okay, but it's good to know..."

Chapter Twenty-two—The Estate Plan

"Of course," Dan continued, "simple solutions work well for you because your lives stayed straight forward. This area gets really complicated with divorces and blended families—those types of challenges need expert help . . ."

"So—we're good?"

"Maybe. Maybe not. What's your biggest asset?"

Paul thought before answering—he wanted to be sure he was right. "There's very little in our personal names—just the house as well as the shares of our holding company . . ."

"Okay—have you thought of what would happen if you both died tomorrow?"

Paul shook his head. "Not really—I guess the kids would inherit the shares and house, and continue on . . ."

Dan's eyebrows shot up. "Actually, it would be a bit of a mess—your kids would be trying to run a plumbing company."

"But let's be more optimistic—say we sell the company to employees five years from now, and I die five years after that. Assume Mandy dies a year later and, at that time, the holding company is worth 10 million . . ."

"Fair enough. First, the easy part, tax-wise—when you die in ten years and leave everything to Mandy, it's almost like nothing happened. The shares of the holding company probably cost you a nominal amount—maybe ten bucks. Mandy just gets the shares at your cost . . ."

Mandy perked up when she heard her name. "I suppose a lot of tax gets triggered when I die . . ."

"You're right—and if your kids don't get expert help, it will be very ugly . . ."

"In what way?"

"Well, your last personal tax return has a 10 million dollar capital gain—half goes into income, so that's 5 million. If your overall personal tax rate is 40%, that's 2 million of tax due—the kids can sell the house to pay that tax . . ."

"So, Paul commented, "they each get 5 million. That's pretty good, don't you think?"

"It seems that way, but I can see a couple of disappointments. First, to make things easy, say the company only had 10 million of cash, and your kids took a few years to wind it up by paying huge dividends. The personal tax could be around 1.5 to 1.8 million—each."

"That's crazy!" Are you saying Mandy's tax is 2 million, and the kids pay another 3 million? That's half the value of the company!"

Mandy was stunned! "Surely, it's double taxation!"

"You're right—but there are a couple of solutions, and I'll give you the simplest. If your kids got good help, the advisors could get them to wind down the company within one year of Mandy's death. The kids still pay the tax on the dividend of 3 million, but, by quickly winding up, the capital gain in Mandy's return should be eliminated . . ."

Mandy thought about that. "So, the kids save 2 million in taxes just because they wound up the company quickly. But, you said there was another solution . . ."

Dan nodded. "Right—odds are the holding company has a variety of assets. Say you had a commercial building that cost 1 million, and is now worth 3 million. The kids could sell it to an outsider, or buy it themselves—but, either way, the tax is going to be triggered. Remember—they have to get all of this done within one year of your death, Mandy . . ."

Chapter Twenty-two—The Estate Plan

Mandy was still stunned. "Gosh! This comes as a bit of a shock—does this happen to most of the somewhat wealthy families owning companies?"

"No—not always. There's another solution that could be put in place, but I think we've had enough serious talk for one night. We can get together again, soon. Now—who wants a beer?"

"Let's set up another meeting to discuss family trusts," Mandy suggested.

"I'm with you," Paul commented. "But I just want to sum up—it sounds as if with estates, the main thing is to get expert help, and put the documents we need in place. Overall, it sounds like KISS is a good objective—keep it simple stupid. But, as far as planning goes, the idea is to know just what's likely to happen when you and your spouse die. If it sounds reasonable, then we're in pretty good shape. But, if something doesn't sound right, or it sounds unexpectedly nasty, then we need to deal with it . . ."

"Correct—now are you ready for that beer?"

Chapter Twenty-three

Family Trusts

When Paul and Mandy left Dan's that evening, they weren't too thrilled by what they learned about estate planning. "It seems," Paul commented to his wife, "there has to be some other vehicle..."

"I think we should investigate family trusts..."

"Family trusts? Where did you hear about those?"

"Yep—I was talking to Silvie the other day, and I told her we're beginning our estate planning. She asked if we considered a family trust..."

"Did she tell you anything about them?"

"No—but she did recommend someone we can talk to, though..."

"Maybe I should talk to Dan first . . ."

Mandy grinned at her husband. "Maybe you should . . ."

****

Mandy made sandwiches for the guys before leaving for the office. Ever since the kids were little, she arrived at work after rush-hour traffic—back then, it was the easiest way to get the kids where they needed to go. Now, she arrived later because it was more relaxing.

Paul kissed his wife just as Dan strode up the walk. "Let's go out to get a bite tonight," Paul suggested as she grabbed her keys.

"Perfect—how about 6:30?"

"Works for me!" Paul watched as Mandy waved to Dan, her smile warm and friendly.

"I'll make sure he takes notes," Dan called to her as he greeted his ex-neighbor with a handshake.

"I need to take notes," Paul laughed. "Thanks for taking the time, again—since our last meeting, I tried Google searches, and I'm confused . . ."

"It can be pretty intimidating, that's for sure!"

Chapter Twenty-three—Family Trusts

Both men made themselves comfortable in front of a platter of sandwiches, and two ice cold beers. "I suggest we ignore all the technical stuff—let's talk about what a trust can do for you . . ."

"Sounds good—why don't we stick to the example you gave us before. Let's say our company is worth roughly 7 million today, but will climb in value to about 10 million in 10 years. Before, we assumed Mandy and I died young, and the kids were facing a tax bill of 3 million or more, even if they handled things well . . ."

Dan nodded. "Good suggestion—first, let's talk about the rights your shares have. I know that sounds strange, but it's very relevant. Right now, there's only one kind of share issued, and you and Mandy have the right to vote, receive dividends, receive the existing value upon winding up, and the right to enjoy any future growth in value."

"Right—but I understand that isn't always the case. Can't different shares have different rights?"

"Yes—normally, the first step in a plan like this is to split up those rights. You and Mandy would get new shares with the right to vote as well as the right to the existing value. However, another new share that has the right to all future growth in value would be set up. Those growth shares are considered by CRA to only have nominal value."

"So we would give those shares to our kids?"

"Not quite—it's a bit more complicated. A trust should be set up and it will have a bank account, filing a tax return every year. What happens is the trust buys the growth shares for nominal value, and the trust has various beneficiaries—that means they can benefit from anything the trust receives. Obviously, your kids are beneficiaries, but others might be included, as well. In twenty-one years, at the latest, you decide whether the kids will get those growth shares in their personal names—that happens at no tax cost. In the meantime, say one of the kids gets married, but the marriage doesn't work out—so far, the courts rule this potential chance of getting shares isn't an asset they have to share with their ex . . ."

Paul thought for a minutes. "And, I suppose if one of kids went off the deep end—got into drugs or something—we could decide to not give them the shares . . ."

"That's right."

"But, who gets the dividends? I imagine we keep that, right? But what about the shares the trust owns? Can those shares get dividends, as well?"

"Yes—but, typically, you only pay dividends to the trust if at least one of the kids is 18. The trust would pass that dividend on to that child—maybe to help them pay for school, or raise a down payment on a house. Going this route might save some income tax vs. just giving them a personal gift . . ."

"So—if I understand you correctly—our shares don't grow. They're frozen at a value of 7 million . . ."

"That's right—professionals call it an estate freeze."

"But the family is stuck paying the tax on the existing value . . ."

"It's better than that—let's say you and Mandy take out $200,000 a year from the company. Instead of paying you dividends, your company could buy back $200,000 of shares each year, and cancel them. Technically, this is called redeeming the shares, and these redemptions are taxed like a dividend—but, the 7 million of shares you own is diminishing. If the company's value isn't changing, when

Chapter Twenty-three—Family Trusts

your shares go down, shares the trust owns go up . . ."

"So if we lived 10 years, we could redeem 2 million of the 7 million?"

"Right—and, if you both lived 35 years, you could redeem the whole 7 million."

Paul still looked a little confused. "So that 3 million the kids were going to pay in tax when Mandy died just disappears?"

Dan nodded. "Sort of—since all the shares Mandy and you owned have been redeemed, no asset is left in your name. But, of course, the value is still there—it just shifted to the shares the trust owns. Maybe by the time you die, your children own those shares." Dan took a bite of his sandwich, then a swig of beer. "In effect, you delay the tax by an entire generation . . ."

"Can our kids do something similar by pushing the tax off to our grandchildren?"

"Maybe—but there isn't a guarantee. Remember—tax laws and circumstances can change."

Paul shook his head. "Now it seems there's always a downside to everything . . ."

Dan grinned at his friend. "That's right—your life is now a bit more confusing and expensive. You face fees for an extra bank account, and you have the costs of filing another tax return each year. And, the other issue is you need to make a decision within 21 years about who gets the shares. Your kids will only be in their mid-30's, and you and Mandy will only be in your mid-60's. It wouldn't be a terrible idea to hold off on this plan for 10 years or so—it could make the taxes worse, but you'll have more time to think about it."

"Maybe that's what we should do—think about it. But it sounds pretty inflexible..."

"Don't conclude that too quick—it would be best to meet with a tax specialist. You'll find these trusts have lots of options..."

"I admit it's easy to see how valuable they can be. Putting off 3 million of tax is pretty good—at 5%, our kids could be making at income of $75,000 each just because the tax was deferred..."

Dan agreed. "And it's nice to show the kids down the road you were doing all you could to take care of them."

Paul was quiet for a moment. "You know, Dan, Mandy and I were just talking last night about what a journey this has been. When we met you twenty years ago, we were living modestly, saving hard to pay off our house, and worrying about how we might ever be able to retire. And, here we are—20 years later—looking at a family trust to enable a 3 million dollar tax deferral." He looked at his friend. "We've been lucky..."

"Lucky? Maybe. But, I say you did a wonderful job of taking advantage of the opportunities you had. You have always lived well within your means, and you have been curious what advisors might have to say—that's important!"

"I couldn't have done it without you..." Paul raised his beer. "Cheers!"

Acknowledgments

First, I have to acknowledge the source of most of this material—I had the distinct privilege of working with and learning from so many talented Chartered Accountants in my professional career.

Second, I want to thank the gang at Raintree Financial Solutions, the home of my comparatively short second career. This material first appeared as chapters in their weekly newsletter—without a weekly deadline, this book would not exist!

Third, to my lovely and talented spouse and family—Marilyn, Kevin, Thea, Craig, Kaitlyn, Sarah, and Julia. Your diverse skills humble me, and round out my life (OT, CFA, CA, LLB, artist, and biologist).

And, yes, for this book—and, clearly the most relevant—the owner of a plumbing company.

Professional Acknowledgments

Chrysalis Publishing Author Services

L.A. O'Neil, Editor
www.chrysalis-pub.com
chrysalispub@gmail.com

Cover Art Design

Jen Kramp Studios
Jen Kramp, Cover Designer
jenkramp@gmail.com

Made in the USA
Charleston, SC
15 November 2016